W9-AZP-161

NoLex 4/14

PEACHTREE CITY
PLAN TO STAY™

THE ILLUSTRATED HISTORY OF THE WORLD

The Dark Ages

PREFACE

*T*he Illustrated History of the World is a unique series of eight volumes covering the entire scope of human history, from the days of the nomadic hunters up to the present. Each volume surveys significant events and personages, key political and economic developments, and the critical forces that inspired change, in both institutions and the everyday life of people around the globe.

The books are organized on a spread-by-spread basis, allowing ease of access and depth of coverage on a wide range of fascinating topics and time periods within any one volume. Each spread serves as a kind of mini-essay, in words and pictures, of its subject. The text—cogent, concise and lively—is supplemented by an impressive array of illustrations (original art, full-color photographs, maps, diagrams) and features (glossary, index, time charts, further reading listings). Taking into account the new emphasis on multicultural education, special care has been given to presenting a balanced portrait of world history: the volumes in the series explore all civilizations— whether it's the Mayans in Mexico, the Shoguns in Japan or the Sumerians in the Middle East.

3

The Dark Ages

Tony Gregory

☑ Facts On File

Facts On File, Inc.
460 Park Avenue South
New York NY 10016

Library of Congress CIP data available upon request
from Facts on File

Gregory, Tony, 1948–
The Dark Ages / Tony Gregory.
p.   cm.
(The illustrated history of the world)
Includes bibliographical references and index.
Summary: Explores the history of the world, from the fall of Rome
to the rise of Islam, discussing such areas as Europe, the
Mediterranean, the Far East, and the Americas.
ISBN 0-8160-2787-0
1. Middle Ages—Juvenile literature.
[1. Middle Ages.] I. Title.
II. Series: Illustrated history of the world
(New York, N.Y.)
D117.074 1992
909.07—dc20
91-43093
CIP
AC

ISBN 0 8160 2787 0

Facts On File books are available at special discounts when purchased
in bulk quantities for businesses, associations, institutions or sales
promotions. Please call our Special Sales Department in New York at
212/683-2244 (dial 800/322-8755 except in NY, AK or HI).

Designed by Hammond Hammond
Composition by Goodfellow and Egan Ltd, Cambridge
Printed and Bound by BPCC Hazell Books, Paulton and Aylesbury

10 9 8 7 6 5 4 3 2 1

This book is printed on acid-free paper.

First Published in Great Britain in 1991 by
Simon and Schuster Young Books

CONTENTS

INTRODUCTION

The period between about AD 400 and AD 1000 is often called 'The Dark Ages.' It was a time when many of the civilizations of the ancient world had collapsed. But it was not really an 'Age of Darkness,' it was more an 'Age of Change.'

Because many of the ancient civilizations had collapsed, we do not have many histories for this period. So it is somewhat different from the Roman Empire that went before, when Roman historians wrote hundreds of accounts of their world and their history.

For the Dark Ages, we have another rich source of information—archaeology. Archaeological excavations and discoveries tell us an enormous amount about what happened. The faint strains of wood in the ground show us what Anglo-Saxon houses looked like, and the huge ruins in the jungles of Cambodia and Central America allow us to reconstruct the cities of the Khmer and the Maya. The Vikings come to life from discoveries of their weapons, their ornaments, and even their great wooden ships.

The histories that we have, and the evidence of archaeology, tell us that many of the changes of the Dark Ages happened because people were on the move. The origin of the greatest of these movements was the great plains of eastern Asia, around Mongolia and northern China. The nomadic tribes burst out of their homelands and spilled out in all directions; other tribes that were in their way were conquered or pushed in front of them.

To the east, west and south, the effects of these movements were felt. The great empires of China, India, Persia, Constantinople and Rome all suffered at the hands of these restless tribes.

But other things were moving too. The Dark Ages was a period of great religious activity. The civilizations of Central and South America, and of Southeast Asia, were based around temples and religious centers. Hinduism, Buddhism and Christianity were spread far afield by missionaries and armies, and it was during this era that the fourth of the world's great religions appeared—Islam.

By the end of the Dark Ages, most traces of the ancient world had been swept away; what replaced it were the foundations of the Middle Ages and the world that we know today.

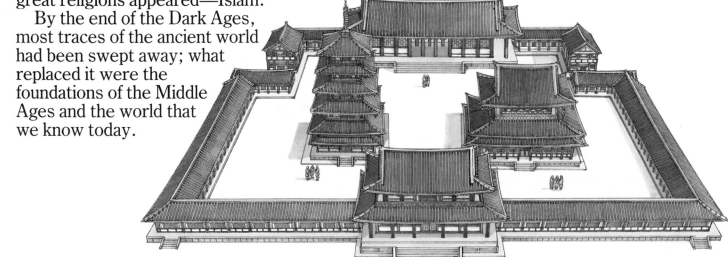

Europe in AD 737

▨ Saxon lands		▨ Lombard Kingdom	
▨ Viking homeland		▨ Byzantine Empire	
▨ Frankish Kingdom		▨ Umayyad Caliphate	

SCANDINAVIA

BERGEN

BRITAIN

LONDON

COLOGNE

ATLANTIC
OCEAN

PARIS

FRANCE

VENICE

RAVENNA

HUNGARY

SPAIN

ITALY   CONSTANTINOPLE

BLACK SEA

CASPIAN
SEA

SAMARKAND

CORDOBA

TURKEY

NORTH AFRICA

SYRIA

MEDITERRANEAN SEA

DAMASCUS

ALEXANDRIA

PART ONE

Europe in Confusion

The map on this page shows the way that Europe looked during the Dark Ages–and it is in Europe that the term, 'Dark Ages,' is most appropriate. For many centuries the Roman Empire had ruled half of Europe as well as parts of Asia and Africa.

THE END OF THE ROMAN EMPIRE People of the Asian steppes began to move southward. They traveled distances in search of land, a search that eventually led to their conquering the Roman Empire. How did it happen? Was it just because Roman armies collapsed and tribes broke in? No, of course it was more complicated than this. The Roman Empire was held together by its administration, roads, seaways and trade as much as by its armies. The Emperor in Rome could send instructions to his generals in Britain or Iraq by way of his official couriers on the Roman roads. Civil servants all over the empire saw that these roads were maintained, bridges built and taxes collected to pay for it all. Food for Rome was brought in ships from as far as Egypt, and the Mediterranean was busy with traders carrying essentials and luxuries from one end of the empire to the other.

NEW PEOPLES The new peoples who took over the old Roman Empire were very different. They were small tribes, who were often at war with each other. Their aim was to carve new land for themselves out of the Empire. During the Dark Ages these tribes gradually turned into settled kingdoms.

Some swallowed up their neighbors to found larger kingdoms, like England. Others, like the Franks, who turned Roman Gaul into Medieval France, became superpowers.

Charlemagne, the greatest of the Frankish kings, founded his Holy Roman Empire to succeed the old one.

THE SPREAD OF CHRISTIANITY Religion was one of the driving forces of the age: the invading tribes were pagans, but the Christian Church survived the collapse of the Roman Empire and quickly converted them. Missionaries went out in all directions to preach to others, and traveled further afield until even the Vikings in Scandinavia became Christian. Between them, the Christian Church and the new kingdoms laid the foundations of modern Europe.

The End of Roman Dominance
STIRRINGS ON THE STEPPES

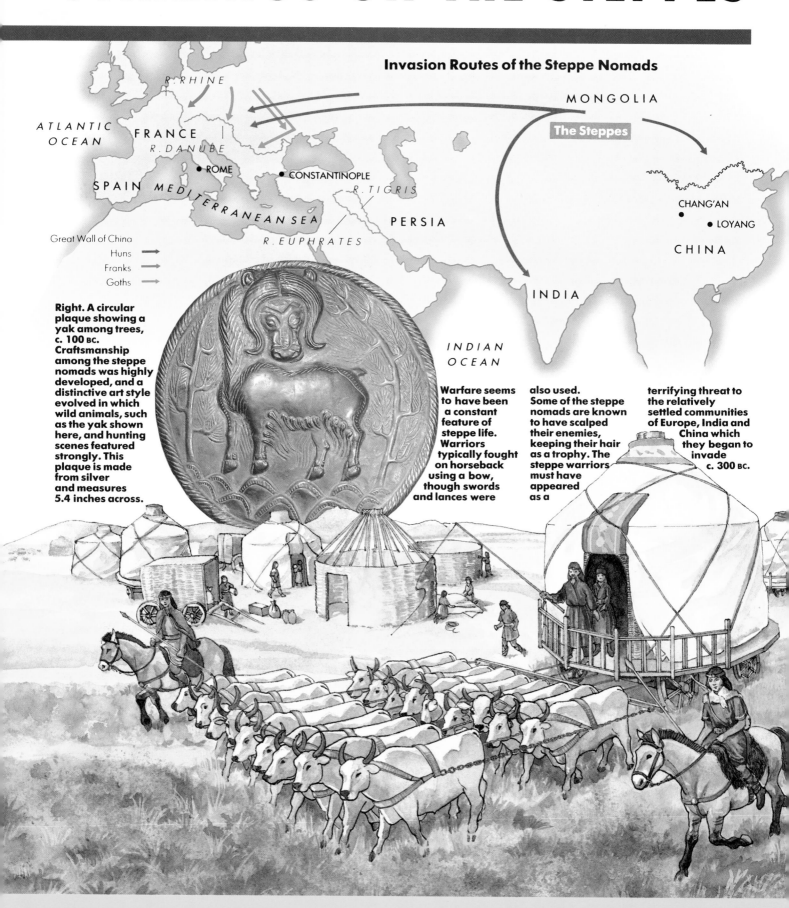

Invasion Routes of the Steppe Nomads

R. RHINE

MONGOLIA

ATLANTIC OCEAN

FRANCE

The Steppes

R. DANUBE

• ROME

• CONSTANTINOPLE

SPAIN

MEDITERRANEAN SEA

R. TIGRIS

CHANG'AN

• LOYANG

PERSIA

R. EUPHRATES

CHINA

Great Wall of China

Huns →
Franks →
Goths →

INDIA

INDIAN OCEAN

Right. A circular plaque showing a yak among trees, c. 100 BC. Craftsmanship among the steppe nomads was highly developed, and a distinctive art style evolved in which wild animals, such as the yak shown here, and hunting scenes featured strongly. This plaque is made from silver and measures 5.4 inches across.

Warfare seems to have been a constant feature of steppe life. Warriors typically fought on horseback using a bow, though swords and lances were also used. Some of the steppe nomads are known to have scalped their enemies, keeping their hair as a trophy. The steppe warriors must have appeared as a terrifying threat to the relatively settled communities of Europe, India and China which they began to invade c. 300 BC.

Imagine a flat plain as far as your eye can see, covered in grass like a great green ocean. The nearest hills are hundreds of miles away, and trees are very scarce. This is the steppe country, from Hungary to the north of China, 4000 miles of grass.

THE TRIBES OF THE STEPPES Fifteen hundred years ago, the empires of Rome and Persia were getting old; but on the steppes the tribes were young and full of life. The world was about to undergo an enormous change.

Hundreds of thousands of people, perhaps millions, lived on these plains. Some, like the Alans, were closely related to the Persians. Others, like the Huns, were much more like the Chinese, and looked very Asiatic. They spent their lives on the move: their homes were wagons pulled by oxen, sometimes with huge woollen tents on board. They depended for their livelihood on their flocks and herds, cattle, sheep and most especially, horses. Everyone rode: men, women and children, and horses provided milk, meat and skins as well.

THE DOMINO EFFECT This nomadic way of life was well organized; each tribe had its own land, and it moved with its animals to different areas at different times of the year. In the winter, southward to escape the cold, and in the summer, northward to follow the sprouting grass. But it would only take one tribe to break the pattern, to try to move into its neighbor's land, and the system would break down, each tribe pushing its neighbor out of the way.

Somehow, perhaps around AD 200, this had started to happen. A hundred years later it was in full swing. Perhaps there were some particularly cold winters or hot dry summers north of China, and the tribes started to move out looking for better land. In Asia, they started to

This section of Trajan's column depicts the cavalry of the Samartians, one of the steppe tribes that attacked the Roman Empire.

move south toward Persia and India, and east into China, and the ancient civilizations started to weaken.

Others headed west, through Russia into Europe. Here, from Germany to Hungary, there was already restlessness. Tribes of Germanic people, called Franks, Lombards, Vandals, Visigoths (West Goths) and Ostrogoths (East Goths) were on the move themselves. For 100 years or more they had looked jealously at the rich lands of the Roman empire, separated from them by the River Rhine and the River Danube and protected by the Roman armies. They had already been raiding the Roman empire, but now as the eastern tribes pressed on them, their raids became more determined.

Owing to constant movement in search of new pasture, the steppe nomads have left very few settlement remains. As they moved from one area of good pasture to the next, some tribes mounted their woollen tents, called 'yurts', onto wagons. Teams of oxen were used to move these early 'mobile homes'.

THE OLD EMPIRES

This rock relief shows the Persian King Shapur I in triumph over the defeated Roman Emperor Valerian.

By now the Romans had ruled most of the Mediterranean area for more than 700 years. France (Gaul to the Romans) had been Roman for more than 400 years and Britain (or Britannia) for 350 years. It was an old empire and cracks were starting to show.

THE PERSIANS Further to the east in Mesopotamia (modern Iraq) and Persia (Iran) there had been civilization for over 3000 years and many empires had risen and fallen–Sumerian, Assyrian, Babylonian and

Parthian. Now the Persians ruled from Iraq to Afghanistan and defended their borders with an army of heavily armed cavalry. These soldiers, archers and lancers in chain-mail shirts and steel helmets, were a match for the Romans.

The religion of the Persians was *Zoroastrianism*, names after their prophet Zoroaster. They worshipped the good god Ormuzd, who was constantly struggling with Ahriman, the evil one. In this way their religion and Christianity had a lot in common. But to the Zoroastrians earth, air, fire and water were sacred, and must not be polluted. To avoid polluting the earth, dead bodies were not buried, but laid out on the top of high wooden towers, to be eaten by vultures and eagles.

To the east, the Persian frontiers were menaced by the tribes of the steppes. In the west there was almost continuous war with Rome; their battlegrounds were Syria, Turkey and Iraq, where Roman and Persian armies fought and died in the deserts.

THE ROMANS Persia was not Rome's only enemy. There had been wars along the northern frontiers of the Roman Empire for many years too. Germanic tribes had

The Roman and Persian Empires

Both the Roman and Persian Empires covered vast areas. The cultural heritage left behind by these Empires after their falls includes, amongst many other things, some beautiful buildings. Shown below are reconstructions of the Arch of Constantine in Rome and the remains of the Taq-i-Kisra palace in Ctesiphon (present-day Baghdad).

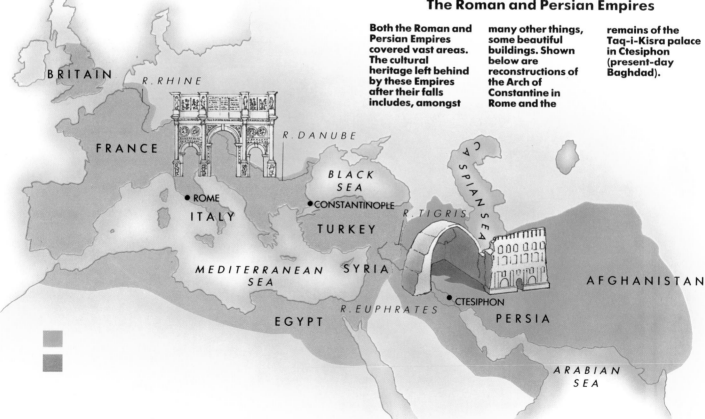

been crossing the Rivers Rhine and Danube, which formed the empire's frontier, to burn and destroy the land. Often the results were disastrous for Rome. Refugees fled from the frontier provinces, from Austria, Yugoslavia, Hungary and Bulgaria (called Noricum, Illyricum, Pannonia and Moesia by the Romans). These were the areas where Rome recruited its best soldiers. In the great battles of this period, tens of thousands of soldiers died, and understandably young men were reluctant to join the army. So how could Rome recruit more troops?

The answer was found in the German tribes themselves. Many of them crossed into the empire and settled as allies in the frontier areas. Here they provided recruits for the army, a solution which worked for some time. Gradually the tribesmen became more and more important to Rome, but they could also cause trouble.

Trouble could come from the army itself, too. Generals, in command of thousands of victorious soldiers, easily became over-ambitious, and had their men declare them emperor in competition to the official ruler. So *civil wars* were not uncommon, and did as much to destroy the empire as wars against invaders.

RELIGION IN THE ROMAN EMPIRE Religion was another source of trouble. In the fourth century AD Christianity became the Empire's main religion, but it was one of many varieties. Different groups had different beliefs, often about very minor details; the differences came out in riots, bloodshed and civil war.

Zoroastrianism

The central prophet of this ancient Persian religion was called Zoroaster. He probably lived around 600 BC. Zoroastrians believe that the prophet was chosen by God to receive his unique revelation. This is contained in 17 hymns, called the *Gathas*.

Fire is the focus of Zoroastrian rites, and many fire temples have been built, such as the one shown below. In such temples, a sacred fire is kept burning in a large vessel, sometimes as high as 2.2 yards. The temples are totally bare except for the fire which represents the living image of God.

1 Around AD 50, the Tiahuanaco and Huari Empires began to dominate much of the central and southern Andes in South America. Although the two civilizations were about 450 miles apart, they were most certainly in contact. They shared an art style and perhaps their religion. Both expanded their empires at the same time, becoming more powerful. Both civilizations had died out by AD 1000.

2 Around AD 400, the city of Jenne-jeno, situated on an island in the River Niger, began to be settled. It is the oldest known city of the Sahara Desert. The city wall, built between AD 400–800, was up to 12 yards wide and had a circumference of 1.2 miles. The city was a center for local trade. Iron ore and grinding stones were imported, and food, especially fish and cereals, was exported to the new towns emerging on the fringes of the desert.

Key Dates

AD 260	Roman Emperor Valerian defeated by Persian King Shapur I
AD 298	30 years' peace treaty between King Narses and Emperor Galerius
AD 363	Emperor Julian invades Persia. Romans win battle of Ctesiphon
AD 364	30 years' peace treaty signed between Shapur II and Emperor Jovian

This coin of the Roman Emperor Magnus Maximus (left) and silver dish showing a typical Persian king contrast the different artistic styles of the two empires.

AD 527–32	War between Emperor Justinian of Byzantium and King Kavadh of Persia
AD 571–591	War between Persia and Byzantium
AD 573	Persians invade Syria
AD 603	Persians invade Byzantine Empire
AD 622	Heraclius, Emperor of Byzantium, attacks Persia
AD 626	Persians besiege Byzantium
AD 627	Byzantines invade Persia
AD 628	Peace signed between Persians and Byzantines
AD 636–648	Persian Empire falls to the Arabs

THE INVADERS

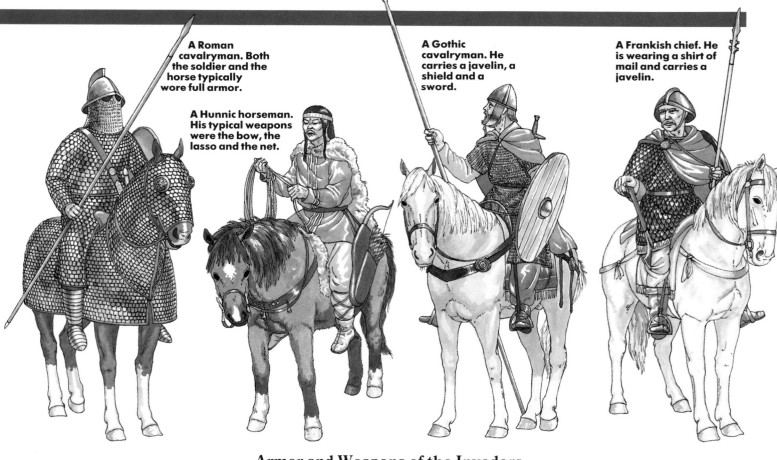

A Roman cavalryman. Both the soldier and the horse typically wore full armor.

A Hunnic horseman. His typical weapons were the bow, the lasso and the net.

A Gothic cavalryman. He carries a javelin, a shield and a sword.

A Frankish chief. He is wearing a shirt of mail and carries a javelin.

Armor and Weapons of the Invaders

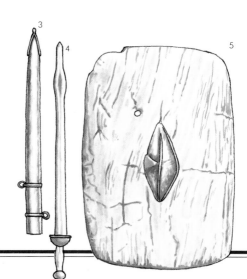

Despite being less well-equipped, the invading armies proved to be very effective in defeating the Roman army.

The Huns, in particular, were superb horsemen and had mastered the use of the bow and arrow. To the Romans, they appeared to live on horseback: 'They are unable to put their feet on the ground: they live and sleep on their horses,' said one Roman historian.

The main weapons of the Franks and Goths were the sword and the javelin. Body armor was rarely worn, and probably only chiefs used it. Ordinary soldiers entered battle naked or clad only in a cloak, or in trousers. Their main means of defense was the shield. These were usually made of wood with an iron boss in the center.

1,2: two examples of the barbed javelins used particularly by the Franks.
3,4: typical Frankish double-edged sword and sheath, fashioned after the Roman design.

5: rectangular wooden shield with a central iron boss.
6: a 'franciska', or throwing axe. Such axes would be hurled at the enemy immediately before contact, and proved extremely effective.

Some of the tribes that threatened the Roman frontiers were Christians; they had been converted by Roman missionaries. Others continued their traditional *pagan* worship. But they were all regarded by the Romans as *barbarians*. This is an interesting word, that was originally used by the Greeks to mean everyone who did not speak Greek; their language, the Greeks thought, sounded like 'ba-ba-ba.' The Romans adopted this, and to them, any people outside the empire, whether they were nomadic Huns or imperial Persians, became 'barbarians.'

INVADING THE EMPIRE Barbarians came at Rome all along the northern frontier, Franks over the Rhine and Goths, Alans and Huns across the Danube. They were very different tribes, but they shared one thing–the use of the horse for war. This had originally started with the tribes of the steppes; Huns and their relatives spent a great deal of time on the backs of their small shaggy ponies, and children learned to ride at the same time that they learned to walk.

DIFFERENCES IN MILITARY TACTICS For centuries the Roman army had relied on its footsoldiers, the heavily armed legionnaires, but they now suffered heavy losses at the hands of Gothic and Hunnish *cavalry*. They soon learned the lesson, and by the fourth century the Roman armys had its own cavalry.

In AD 378 a great battle was fought at Adrianople in Bulgaria, when the Goths wiped out most of the Roman army. It was the Gothic cavalry that made the difference. They sat in saddles, with their feet firmly anchored in stirrups, and charged with lances. It was the saddle and the stirrup, which were far superior to the equipment of the Roman cavalry, that made the difference.

THE WARRIOR TRIBES The Roman world was divided into soldiers who fought and civilians who did not. In the barbarian tribes it was different: all free men were warriors. Chiefs and nobles had bands of young fighting men around them. These fighting men owed

Arts and Crafts of the Barbarians

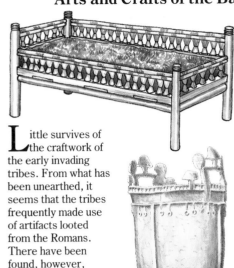

Little survives of the craftwork of the early invading tribes. From what has been unearthed, it seems that the tribes frequently made use of artifacts looted from the Romans. There have been found, however, some beautiful pieces of metalwork and woodwork which attest to their artistic skills.

Above left. A Frankish bed, made for a boy. It is made of wood and is decorated with balusters.
Above right. A bird brooch of Frankish type.
Left. A Hunnic bronze stewpot from the fifth century AD.

everything to their chief who fed and housed them and led them into battle. The richer and more warlike the chief, the more warriors he supported and the more powerful he became.

So war was a way of life in the tribes. They were restless, always seeking more plunder, more power and more land for their families and their herds.

In some ways, the barbarians seemed to have all the advantages; their cavalry was a formidable weapon, and their way of life encouraged the raiding and warfare which wore down the Roman Empire. But they learned quickly too; tribes who fought in the Roman army were quick to pick up Roman tactics and methods; when the time was convenient, they turned on their old masters, and the Empire seemed powerless before them.

Left. This silver plaque from the fourth century AD depicts the Roman Emperor, Theodosius I, surrounded by German mercenary bodyguards. As the barbarians invaded the Empire, many of them joined the Roman army, as the Romans admired their fighting prowess.

AN EMPIRE DIVIDED

The Roman empire was huge: it stretched more than 4000 miles from Britain to Egypt and from Spain to Iraq. Even with the Roman system of roads and safe seaways it took many days to get a message from the emperor in Rome to a general on the frontier. How could an empire like that be controlled? Generals were all too easily tempted to set themselves up as emperors in revolt.

In AD 286 the emperor Diocletian tried to solve the problem: he split his empire in two. The eastern half was to be ruled by him, from a capital at Nicomedia in Turkey. The western half was given to his co-emperor,

Maximian, who ruled not from Rome but from Milan. This arrangement lasted until AD 323 when Constantine I, Constantine the Great, found himself sole emperor after many years of civil war.

A NEW CAPITAL Constantine set his sons up as caesars, or princes, to help him with the job of running the immense empire. The enemies of Rome were closing in, in Persia and on the River Danube. The emperor had to be in his capital, but near enough to the theaters of war to direct operations. So, where should the capital be?

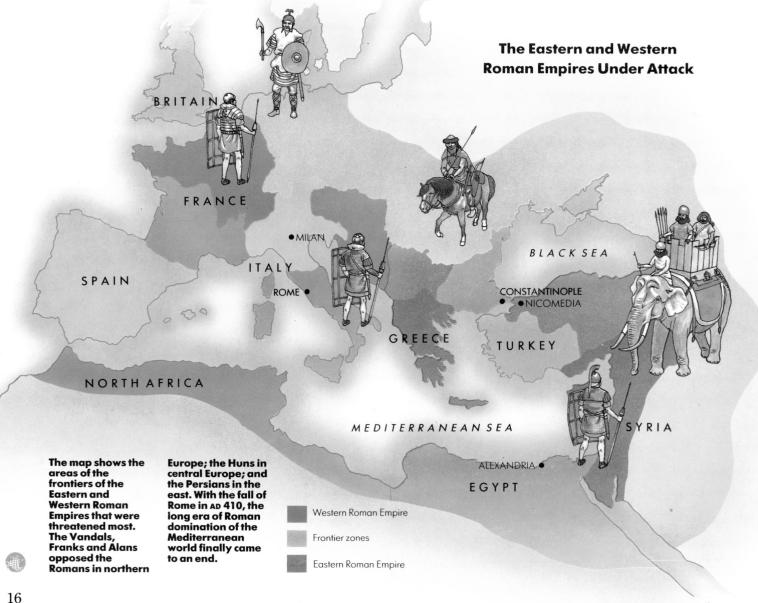

The Eastern and Western Roman Empires Under Attack

The map shows the areas of the frontiers of the Eastern and Western Roman Empires that were threatened most. The Vandals, Franks and Alans opposed the Romans in northern Europe; the Huns in central Europe; and the Persians in the east. With the fall of Rome in AD 410, the long era of Roman domination of the Mediterranean world finally came to an end.

Western Roman Empire

Frontier zones

Eastern Roman Empire

16

On the Bosporus, a narrow channel that separates Europe from Asia, was the old town of Byzantium. Here were the crossroads of the Empire. Constantine dreamed up a scheme to turn this small town into the greatest city in the world. He built palaces, churches, official buildings and houses, and an immense racetrack– the Hippodrome. The greatest works of art of the empire were brought to adorn the new city. At its heart he set up the True Cross, the wooden cross on which Christ was said to have been crucified, brought back from Jerusalem by Constantine's mother Helena.

CONSTANTINOPLE On 11 May AD 330, after 40 days of celebrations, the new city was dedicated, with the name of Constantinople (Greek for 'the city of Constantine'– over the years this name has been changed to Istanbul). Carved on a stone pillar was the slogan 'the new Rome.' But it was a city with a Greek name, and its people spoke Greek.

After AD 334 Constantine became sole ruler of the Roman Empire. Not only was Constantinople called the 'new Rome' it also became the capital of the eastern Empire. Power gradually shifted to the richer eastern Empire at a time when the nomadic and highly mobile people of Eurasia began expanding southward. The Romans of the eastern empire, from the capital at Constantinople, beat back the Goths from the Danube and the Persians from the eastern frontier: the western empire fared much worse.

The Goths turned away from the east: Alaric and his tribes of Visigoths invaded Italy, while another *barbarian* army of Vandals and Alans crossed the frozen River Rhine into France. In AD 410 Alaric captured Rome, the first time that the city had fallen to barbarians for 800 years. The Goths burned and destroyed the city and then marched south. The city of Rome came back to life, but it would never again be the capital of a great empire. From then on, western Europe belonged to the Germanic tribes, and it began to take the form that lives on in modern Europe.

Left. A detail of the obelisk of Theodosius from Constantinople (Istanbul), showing Theodosius holding a wreath for a victorious charioteer. Theodosius was Emperor of the Eastern Empire from AD 379–395.

Above. Constantine I is portrayed here on a gold coin minted at Nicomedia in AD 335. The artist who created the image for the coin intended that Constantine should be seen looking upward. This was so that he should appear 'as though speaking with God' as Eusebius, Constantine's biographer, records.

Right. Bust of the Emperor Diocletian found at Nicomedia. Diocletian's main reform was to divide the Empire in two. He ruled the east from Nicomedia, and Maximian ruled the west from Rome.

17

THE END OF THE WORLD?

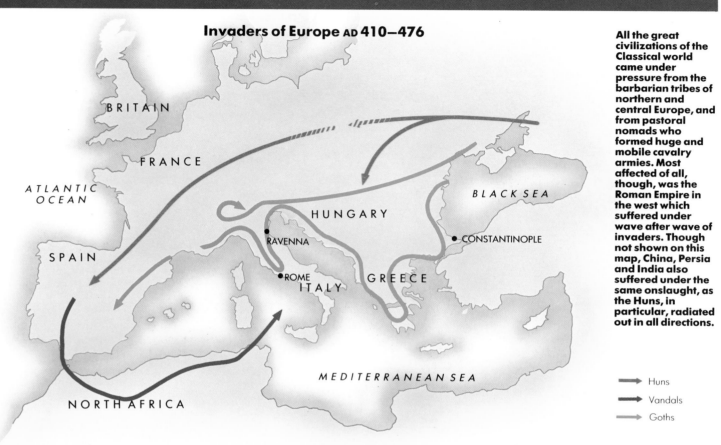

Invaders of Europe AD 410–476

BRITAIN

FRANCE

ATLANTIC OCEAN

SPAIN

RAVENNA

ROME
ITALY

HUNGARY

GREECE

BLACK SEA

CONSTANTINOPLE

MEDITERRANEAN SEA

NORTH AFRICA

→ Huns
→ Vandals
→ Goths

All the great civilizations of the Classical world came under pressure from the barbarian tribes of northern and central Europe, and from pastoral nomads who formed huge and mobile cavalry armies. Most affected of all, though, was the Roman Empire in the west which suffered under wave after wave of invaders. Though not shown on this map, China, Persia and India also suffered under the same onslaught, as the Huns, in particular, radiated out in all directions.

By AD 410 the frontiers of the western empire had crumbled; the Visigoths were in Italy and the Alans and Vandals had taken over France. Also in France were the Franks, tribes from Holland and north Germany who had been given land there by the Roman authorities more than 100 years before. In Britain the Roman army declared its own commander as emperor, Constantine III. He crossed the channel, joined up with the Franks and crushed the Alans and Vandals.

But then, to make things even more confusing, the Visigoths, who had just *sacked* Rome, marched into the south of France and established their own kingdom there. Meanwhile the Alans and Vandals slipped into Spain. There were barbarians all over Europe.

The western Roman empire was now comprised of Italy and parts of North Africa–a poor shadow of what it had once been. It had its capital at Ravenna and was supplied with corn from North Africa. It was small yet still an empire; but not for long.

In AD 429 the Vandals, 80,000 of them under their king, Gaeseric, crossed the straits of Gibraltar by ship

The Fortress of Divitia

The Fortress of Divitia, near modern-day Cologne in Germany, was built on the east bank of the River Rhine to defend the Empire against barbarian attacks. It was large enough to hold a garrison of 900 soldiers.

The Romans built 45 such fortresses on their frontiers. Despite their efforts, the barbarians still managed to go around Roman defenses to attack the Empire.

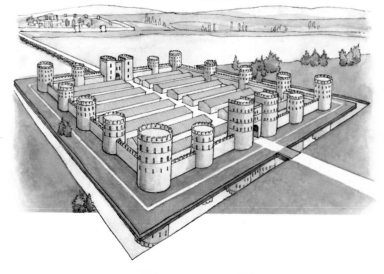

Left. A Visigothic votive crown made in the second half of the seventh century AD. It is made of gold and is inlaid with precious stones. Most of the invading tribes were converted to Christianity. This crown was made by Visigoths who had been converted to Christianity in northern Spain.

Above. A Hunnic brooch depicting a cicada from the fourth/fifth centuries AD. Such brooches were used as a sign of rank among the Huns. It is made from gold and is inlaid with precious stones.

and arrived in Africa. By AD 435 they had captured all the Roman possessions from Morocco to Tunisia. First they tightened the noose on Italy by cutting off the corn supplies, then they raided Italy itself.

ATTILA AND THE HUNS Meanwhile there was another invader at hand, the fiercest and most terrifying of all, the Huns. They had worked their way into Europe and had set themselves up in Hungary under their king Attila, whose name even today is associated with terror and savagery. In AD 451 Attila swept through France until, at the battle of Moirey, he was stopped by an extraordinary allied army–the Roman army from Ravenna, Franks from northern France and Visigoths and Alans from the south. They had all united against the ultimate threat.

Attila was beaten off and had to retreat into Hungary. But the next year he was back, this time in Italy and threatening to destroy Rome. Only the threat of an army from Constantinople, and a personal visit from Pope Leo stopped him. A few months later he was dead, and Europe could breathe easily again.

THE SACK OF ROME But Rome was far from safe. In AD 455, only three years after the Huns had been diverted, the Vandals sailed across from Africa, where they had taken control of all Roman African territories, invaded Italy and sacked Rome. They spared the lives of the inhabitants but looted and destroyed the buildings. Even now their name is used to mean acts of wanton destruction. They soon withdrew, leaving Italy to a Roman emperor, supported by an army of German *mercenaries*. Finally in AD 476 the Roman Emperor, Romulus Augustulus, was deposed and a German king, Odovocar, took over the shadow of the empire.

For centuries Rome had ruled Italy, and Italy had ruled much of the known world; now it was over. The Old World was coming to an end, but a new one was starting: there was a new 'Roman' empire, ruled by 'Roman' emperors, in the east based at Constantinople (modern-day Istanbul). And, more important still, the German tribes that had brought Rome to its knees were creating their own states, laying the foundations of modern Europe.

WRITING, READING AND DIGGING

Much of the history we have knowledge of is due to the painstaking efforts of clergymen such as these. This ivory depicts Pope Gregory who held office from AD 590–604.

WRITTEN HISTORY Some of these books, written out by hand and painstakingly copied by *scribes*, have survived through the centuries, many of them in the libraries of monasteries. The invention of printing made it possible to spread them all over the world. But some have been lost, burnt in fires, or just thrown away, and a part of our memory has gone.

History can also be confusing. Authors disagree with each other and leave us different versions of the same event. Also, depending on their nationality and other factors, authors can use bias in their books to give a more or less favorable version of events. So historians have to untangle a very twisted web to get to the truth. Copying has not helped; imagine that you are a scribe, copying by hand a long and badly written manuscript: you leave parts out; you make mistakes; you even change things, or add your own comments. So there can be many versions of the same history book, each slightly different.

On top of this there were places and times when there were very few historians; this happened in the west of Europe in the fifth, sixth and seventh centuries. So this period of time has come to be called the 'Dark Ages,' not because it was uncultured or backward, but because written information is scarce.

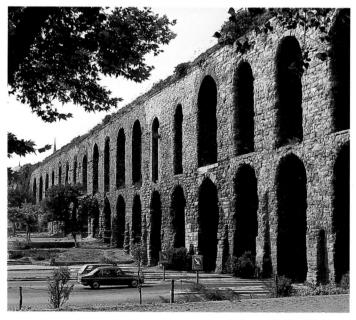

Some buildings have survived almost intact from many hundreds, even thousands, of years ago. The aqueduct of Valens, built in Constantinople (Istanbul) in the fourth century AD has survived particularly well. Large-standing structures such as this can tell us much about earlier times.

We talk confidently about wars and invasions, about the savagery of the Huns, and the destruction caused by the Vandals. But how do we know? Our memories do not reach back that far. But in a way they do.

Historians, passing down knowledge about the past from one generation to the next, give us a sort of memory. For 2500 years history has been written–by Greeks, Romans, Franks, Arabs and all sorts of people– recording the worlds that they knew and the history behind them. These works give us unique insights into the past.

Unearthing an Anglo-Saxon Village

The pictures here show the kind of artifacts archaeologists discover, and how they can put their knowledge to use.

West Stow in Suffolk, England, was home to an Anglo-Saxon village. All the original buildings were made of wood and had thatched roofs, so little trace of them has been left behind.

Skilled archaeological excavation, however, managed to detect the trenches and holes that were dug to take the wooden posts that formed the walls of the buildings.

By digging these out again, archaeologists could tell how the buildings were constructed and were able to build accurate reconstructions.

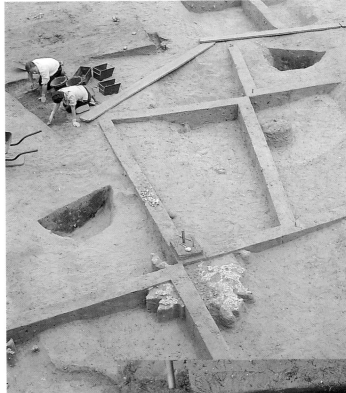

Left. It took painstaking excavation to unearth these Anglo-Saxon foundations at West Stow. Though this may not seem to reveal much about the Anglo-Saxons to the untrained eye, archaeologists were able to piece together the whole structure and shape of the community. Such excavations tell us a great deal about the history of the 'Dark Ages'. Far left. This bone comb was found in an Anglo-Saxon burial at West Stow. A mole had burrowed through the middle. The Anglo-Saxons must have been quite proud of their hair and their appearance.

Left. An Anglo-Saxon house at West Stow constructed on its original site. A house such as this would have accommodated one family.

Above. Near the village at West Stow was a cemetery where the villagers were buried. Several burials like this have been unearthed.

ARCHAEOLOGICAL INVESTIGATIONS So we have to look for another source, and luckily there is a very rich one–archaeology.

This is the investigation of *material remains*–objects that people used, the buildings that they lived in and the remains of the sites where they lived. They might be huge, like the *aqueduct* at Constantinople, or tiny, like coins; but each one has a story to tell.

The stories about ordinary people, Roman citizens or German tribesmen, how and where they lived, what they ate, and so on, can only really come from archaeology. So digging the sites of towns, villages and farms is vital.

They are lying buried, often only a few inches underground. They are there not because they were buried in some catastrophe, but simply because people moved away somewhere else, and the houses fell down; or they built new ones on top and buried the old.

The trash that they left behind, broken pieces of pottery, fragments of jewelry, even charred wood and bone, help archaeologists to put together a picture of how they lived.

Faint traces of the foundations of wooden houses, drainage ditches and pits full of rubbish have as much to tell us as the writings of ancient historians.

New Settlers

ANGLES, SAXONS AND JUTES

This seventh century AD Germanic carving shows Wotan, lord of the Teutonic gods. He was the god of war, and is shown here wearing a helmet and armed with shield, sword and spear.

Right. Anglo-Saxon spearheads found in England. The Saxons were known to be the cruelest of the invaders. Each band followed its war-lord and was eager to fight and die, if necessary, when he died in battle.

who were farmers, sailors and soldiers at the same time.

Their raids probably started in the third century AD, when Roman authorities built forts along the coasts of England and France–the forts of the Saxon Shore. By AD 300 the Saxons were the menace of the North Sea, and in AD 367 they crossed it in force. At the same time, tribes from Scotland and Ireland invaded Roman Britain. Much of the country was devastated. But the invaders, having plundered and destroyed, returned home.

THE URGE TO ROAM Why were the people of Denmark and Germany on the move? It was partly because they were affected by the mood of unrest all around them. But also, as we know from archaeology, living conditions at home were getting worse. Until about AD 200 the weather had been comparatively warm and dry, and farms prospered. Then a colder, wetter period set in and life became much more difficult. There seems to be evidence that the sea began to encroach more and more on the low-lying lands of northern Europe. Food would have been harder to come by; the young men looked overseas, and Britain looked a promising target.

Every year the raids became more destructive. While the Roman Empire was strong they were a nuisance, but little more. Some tribesmen were allowed

W hile the Goths and the other tribes were surging over the old Roman frontiers, the people of the north were restless too.

THE PEOPLES OF NORTHERN EUROPE On the north coast of Holland and Germany were the Frisians and Saxons, and Denmark was home to the Angles and Jutes. They were all Germanic peoples, farmers and seafarers who were intent on adventure and plunder. Summer raiding was probably part of the way of life of their men,

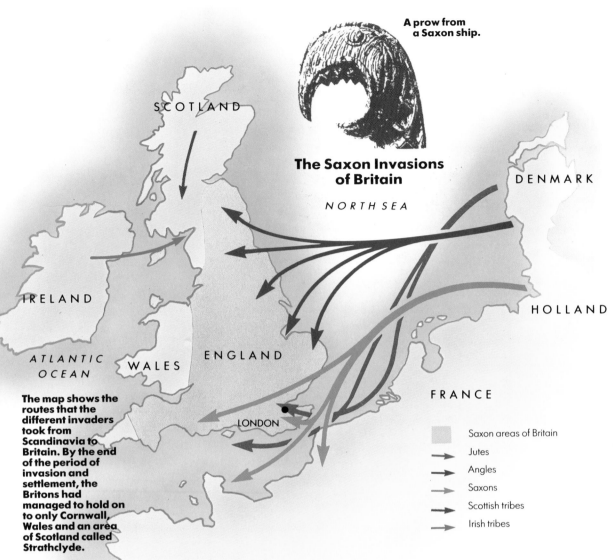

A prow from
a Saxon ship.

**The Saxon Invasions
of Britain**

SCOTLAND

NORTH SEA

DENMARK

IRELAND

ATLANTIC
OCEAN

WALES

ENGLAND

HOLLAND

FRANCE

LONDON

The map shows the
routes that the
different invaders
took from
Scandinavia to
Britain. By the end
of the period of
invasion and
settlement, the
Britons had
managed to hold on
to only Cornwall,
Wales and an area
of Scotland called
Strathclyde.

Saxon areas of Britain

Jutes

Angles

Saxons

Scottish tribes

Irish tribes

The New Language

With the invaders themselves came a new language. The native language of the Anglo-Saxons pushed back the language of the Britons to the Celtic fringes. In the process, it almost totally obliterated the influence of Celtic from what came to be known as 'Old English.'

Today, when using modern English, it is almost impossible to write a sentence without using Anglo-Saxon words. Basic words, such as 'the,' 'is,' and 'you' are Anglo-Saxon in origin. The word 'man' is a descendant of Anglo-Saxon 'mann' and 'house' is derived from 'hus.' Computer analysis of modern English has shown that the 100 most commonly used words are of Anglo-Saxon origin.

to settle in Britain as allied troops. But by AD 410 Britain was the least of the empire's worries. Goths were loose in Italy, and the Romano-Britons had to fend for themselves.

We know little of the details, but we can imagine the raiders getting bolder, and Romano-British troops retreating into the walled towns, leaving the *barbarians* to roam the countryside at will. Soon the towns were captured, or were deserted as civic order collapsed. To add to all this, *plague* and famine came too.

FROM ROMANS TO ANGLO-SAXONS It took 40 or 50 years for the raiders to become settlers, so the change was gradual. By about AD 450 the Angles, Saxons and Jutes (who probably had Frisians with them) were building their farms and villages in Britain; they were the new ruling classes. But ordinary Romano-Britons survived. They simply swapped wealthy Roman bosses for new Germanic ones. They adopted the invaders' languages and customs. Roman Britain became Saxon England.

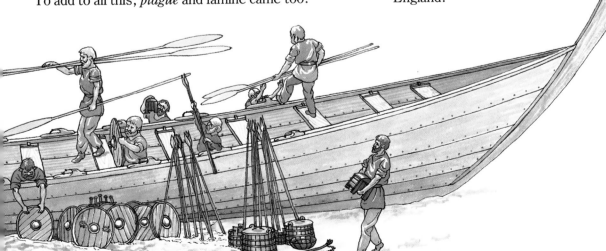

Left. This longboat,
reconstructed from
the remains of a
boat found at
Nydam in Denmark,
is the kind of vessel
in which the Anglo-
Saxon invaders
crossed to Britain.
It was rowed by 14
pairs of oarsmen,
and could carry a
total of 30—40
warriors.

ANGLO-SAXON ENGLAND

By AD 500 the Anglo-Saxons were masters of most of eastern England, but then they met a setback. Around that year they were defeated in battle at Mons Badonicus, somewhere in the southwest of England, by a British war leader, Ambrosius Aurelianus. He was probably just one of a number of British rulers opposing them–another might well have been the legendary King Arthur. It was only a temporary setback, however, and eventually the whole country became Anglo-Saxon.

LIFE IN ENGLAND The old Roman towns, like London and St Albans, were almost deserted. A few of the old buildings were still used, but most were allowed to fall down, and the land was used for fields and gardens. It was out in the countryside that most of the new settlements appeared. These were typically farms and villages like the ones that the tribes had left behind in their homelands.

Here they grew corn and tended herds of cattle, sheep and pigs. The main houses were large timber halls, as big as barns; here the family lived in one end, and used the other end for storage and to keep animals over the winter. Nearby were smaller buildings and sheds, often with wooden floors over pit-like cellars; these were used for storage and as workshops. A pen for animals completed the farm, and nearby there might be a wooden shrine where *pagan* gods were worshipped.

All the men of the community were warriors who could be called to war by their chief. Armed with shields, spears and swords they would march to join the local king.

THE NEW KINGDOMS The settlers had broken up into a host of small states, many of them no bigger than modern English counties. The Jutes took Kent and the Isle of Wight. The Saxons established a number of kingdoms in the rest of southern England, where their names still survive–Essex (East Saxons), Middlesex (Middle Saxons), and Wessex (West Saxons).

To the north were the Angles–the Northfolk (Norfolk) and Southfolk (Suffolk) in East Anglia. There were many small Anglian kingdoms further west and north which, in the sixth century, came together as Mercia and Northumbria. It was a time of warring kings and kingdoms, each one getting the upper hand for a while, and then another taking over. It was not until the ninth century that the kings of Wessex could claim to be the kings of all England.

By now it had become 'England' (Angleland). Germanic languages were spoken almost everywhere, and Germanic laws had replaced Roman ones. The foundations of modern England were being laid.

A typical Saxon village in England had groups of single-roomed buildings for sleeping, workshops and storehouses. Each group was centered around a 'hall' or house/cow shed, such as the one shown here on the far right. There was probably one hall for each family. The whole family met and lived in their hall: uncles and aunts, brothers, sisters and slaves.

King Arthur

F
ew facts are
known about
King Arthur and today
there is still great
debate about whether
he actually ever lived.

Even though King
Arthur's existence
cannot be proved,
what does seem clear
is that around AD 500,
a leader of the Britons
defeated the Anglo-
Saxons.

According to
legend, Arthur, the
son of the British
King, Uther
Pendragon, was
brought up in secret
by the wizard Merlin.
Years later he proved
himself the rightful
King when he alone
was able to pull a
sword out of a block of
stone. The sword was
called 'Excalibur.'
Arthur's royal court
was at Camelot where

he was served by a
company of knights.
They dined at a round
table and often rode
away to carry out
noble deeds.

**Left. The Round
Table in the Great
Hall at Winchester
was once thought to
have been Arthur's
table. We now
know, however,
that it was made in
the thirteenth
century.**

**Below. This site in
South Cadbury in
England is now
commonly
believed to
have been
Arthur's
Camelot.**

THE CELTS

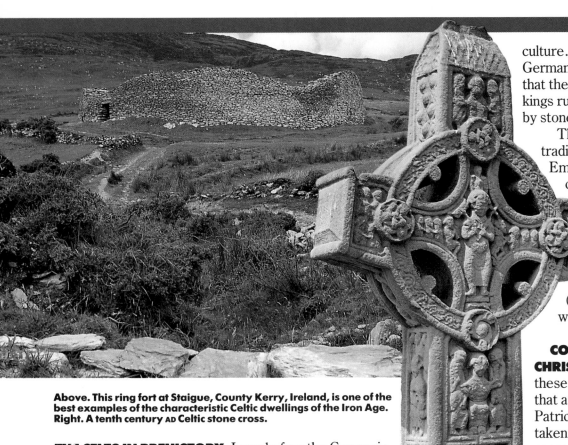

Above. This ring fort at Staigue, County Kerry, Ireland, is one of the best examples of the characteristic Celtic dwellings of the Iron Age. Right. A tenth century AD Celtic stone cross.

THE CELTS IN PREHISTORY Long before the Germanic tribes swept across Europe, others had done the same. The Celts, also known as Gauls and Galatians, spread over the European continent perhaps as much as 3000 years ago. By the height of the Iron Age, between about 600 BC and the time of the Roman Empire, they occupied Britain, Spain, France, south Germany and Czechoslovakia. Also, from time to time they descended on Italy, Greece and Turkey.

They were warlike, colorful and extravagant. At the same time they were great craftsmen in iron and bronze. Their kings held great *barbaric* courts where *bards* regaled feasting warriors with songs and poems of magic and heroes, and with the *epic* tales of their past.

One by one the Celtic tribes fell to the Roman Empire until, by AD 100, only Ireland (where the Scots, or Scotti, lived) and the north of Scotland, home of the Picts, remained independent.

CELTIC IRELAND While their cousins in Britain took on Roman ways, the Irish carried on to develop a very special Celtic culture. Their lives, like those of the Germans, revolved around the duties that they owed to their kings. Celtic kings ruled from strongholds defended by stone walls or earth ramparts.

They carried on the old traditions, raiding the Roman Empire by descending on the west coast of Wales and England. As Roman power declined, Irish successes increased, and they founded settlements in Wales, and in Scotland where their name (Scots) was soon given to the whole country.

CONVERSION TO CHRISTIANITY It was on one of these raids, perhaps around AD 410, that a young Christian Briton called Patrick (Patricius) was captured and taken as a slave to Ireland. He escaped, but went back about AD 432 as one of the earliest Christian *missionaries*. He and his colleagues were spectacularly successful, and soon Christianity was a powerful force in Ireland.

Meanwhile, Anglo-Saxons were taking over England and Christianity was disappearing there. So it was the Irish who, in AD 563, first brought the faith back to Britain. An Irish missionary, Columba, founded a monastery on the isle of Iona, off the west coast of Scotland. Celtic Christianity spread quickly, Eventually Irish monks and their new English converts were traveling throughout western Europe, founding more monasteries abroad.

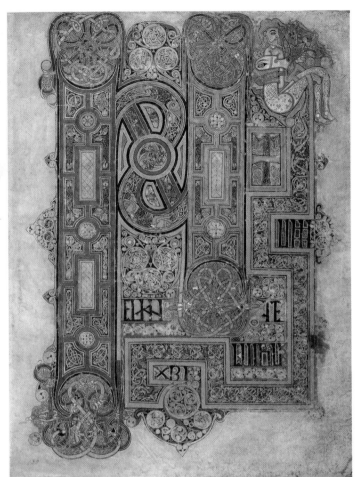

Illuminated Manuscripts

One of the most beautiful art forms to emerge from the Dark Ages is the art of illuminated manuscripts. At a time when life was crude and harsh, when barely one man in a thousand could read or write, monks of the Celtic Church were producing beautifully written and illustrated books.

They worked in tiny unheated cells. They accepted this total lack of comfort because their books were for the glory of God and the Christian religion.

You can see from looking at this page from the Book of Kells, produced in the eighth century AD, just how intricate and fine the monks' work was.

It seems incredible that this could have been produced by hand.

Above. By the mid-fifth century AD, the lands held by the Celts had dwindled to a very small area. Celtic communities had occupied most of western Europe during the first millenium BC. The rise of Rome and frequent invasions by European tribes had beaten the Celts back to the western extremities of the British Isles and France. Today, Celtic heritage is still very much alive in the languages and the folklore of Wales, Scotland, Ireland, and Brittany in western France.

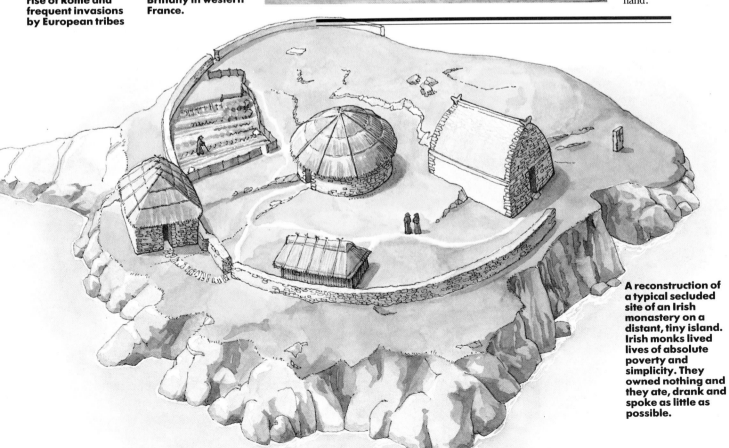

A reconstruction of a typical secluded site of an Irish monastery on a distant, tiny island. Irish monks lived lives of absolute poverty and simplicity. They owned nothing and they ate, drank and spoke as little as possible.

A NEW EUROPE

This front plaque of a gilt bronze helmet, c. AD 600, shows the Lombard King, Agilulf, enthroned and surrounded by courtiers.

By AD 476, the west had settled into a number of more or less stable kingdoms. The Vandals had been established in North Africa since AD 435. The properties of the old Roman landowners there were shared out between the Vandals, but the 'Romans'—mostly Romanized Africans—ran the civil service and worked the land. They lived under Roman law, and the Vandals under Vandal law, side by side.

In Spain and the south of France, the Visigoths used a similar system. Goths were forbidden to marry into the native population and the two peoples were kept separate. Some signs of what the Romans would have called 'civilization' began to appear—the Visigothic laws were translated into Latin, for example.

CHRISTIANS AND ARIANS Like the people of Roman France and Spain, the Franks were Catholics by religion. The Goths and Vandals, on the other hand, had been converted long before to a different brand of Christianity, *Arianism*. To the Catholics, this made them *heretics*. Nearby was another group, the Burgundians. They had converted to Catholicism from Arianism, but this did not save them from the Franks, who did not believe that they had converted quite quickly enough. The Burgundians were taken over in AD 534, and now all that remains is their name, covering an area in southeastern France.

THEODERIC AND ZENO In Italy, Theoderic, king of the Ostrogoths, had murdered Odovacar by treachery, and Italy joined Switzerland and Yugoslavia in his kingdom.

The New Languages of Europe

Latin had been the official language of the Roman Empire. People throughout the empire spoke one of two forms: educated people spoke classical Latin, and ordinary people spoke vernacular Latin.

As invaders settled into the old lands of the Empire, the vernacular Latin spoken in different areas began to be influenced by the languages of the new settlers.

The Franks and Burgundians, for example, who had settled in France, eventually influenced the language so much that by AD 800 an early form of French was being spoken. The Goths and the Lombards in Italy contributed to the emergence of the Italian language.

Other *Romance languages*—those derived from vernacular Latin—include: Spanish, Portuguese and Romanian.

This had the support of the Emperor at Constantinople, Zeno. Theoderic repaid the Emperor's support by continuing the traditions of Rome; under the Visigoths public building in the Roman style, as well as Roman arts and crafts, were encouraged.

But Zeno's support did not last long. In AD 530 an army from Constantinople landed in North Africa, defeated the Vandals and then turned on Italy. Belisarius, the Roman general, seemed about to bring Italy into the Eastern Empire, and for a while Italy was ruled from Constantinople. But this did not last long.

DEAD BUT NOT FORGOTTEN When Lombards invaded Italy from the north in AD 568, the Roman world seemed to be dead—but much of it was still remembered. The

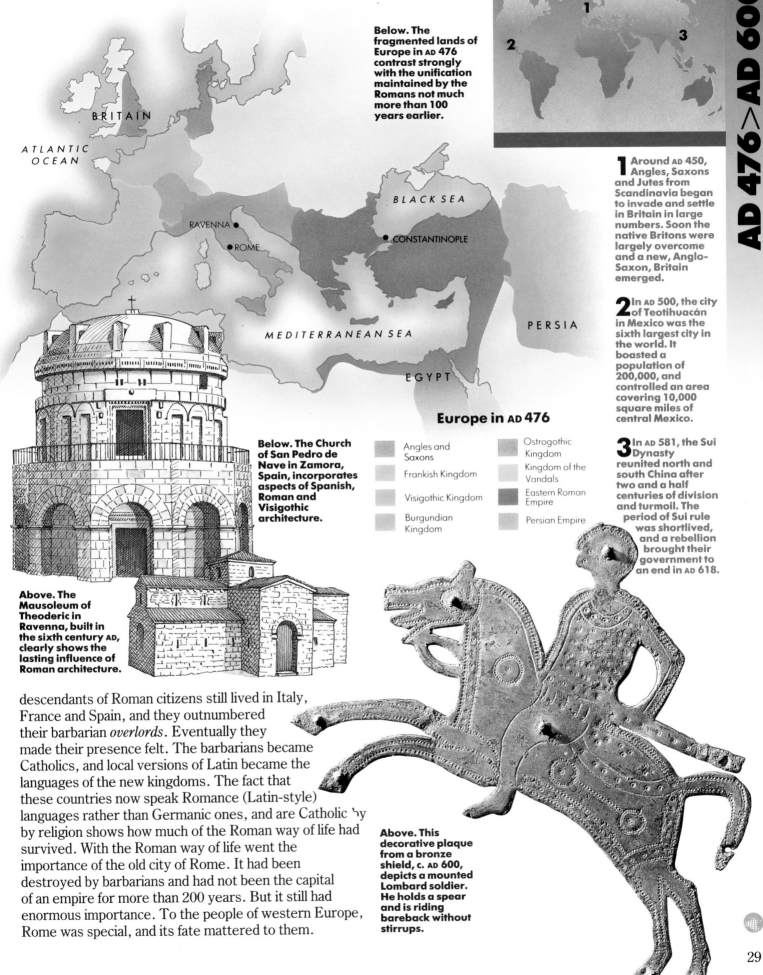

Below. The fragmented lands of Europe in AD 476 contrast strongly with the unification maintained by the Romans not much more than 100 years earlier.

BRITAIN

ATLANTIC OCEAN

BLACK SEA

RAVENNA •

• ROME

• CONSTANTINOPLE

MEDITERRANEAN SEA

PERSIA

EGYPT

Europe in AD 476

Angles and Saxons

Frankish Kingdom

Visigothic Kingdom

Burgundian Kingdom

Ostrogothic Kingdom

Kingdom of the Vandals

Eastern Roman Empire

Persian Empire

1 Around AD 450, Angles, Saxons and Jutes from Scandinavia began to invade and settle in Britain in large numbers. Soon the native Britons were largely overcome and a new, Anglo-Saxon, Britain emerged.

2 In AD 500, the city of Teotihuacán in Mexico was the sixth largest city in the world. It boasted a population of 200,000, and controlled an area covering 10,000 square miles of central Mexico.

3 In AD 581, the Sui Dynasty reunited north and south China after two and a half centuries of division and turmoil. The period of Sui rule was shortlived, and a rebellion brought their government to an end in AD 618.

Below. The Church of San Pedro de Nave in Zamora, Spain, incorporates aspects of Spanish, Roman and Visigothic architecture.

Above. The Mausoleum of Theoderic in Ravenna, built in the sixth century AD, clearly shows the lasting influence of Roman architecture.

descendants of Roman citizens still lived in Italy, France and Spain, and they outnumbered their barbarian *overlords*. Eventually they made their presence felt. The barbarians became Catholics, and local versions of Latin became the languages of the new kingdoms. The fact that these countries now speak Romance (Latin-style) languages rather than Germanic ones, and are Catholic by by religion shows how much of the Roman way of life had survived. With the Roman way of life went the importance of the old city of Rome. It had been destroyed by barbarians and had not been the capital of an empire for more than 200 years. But it still had enormous importance. To the people of western Europe, Rome was special, and its fate mattered to them.

Above. This decorative plaque from a bronze shield, c. AD 600, depicts a mounted Lombard soldier. He holds a spear and is riding bareback without stirrups.

THE CHURCH

As Irish Christianity spread southward in Britain, Catholicism came north to meet it. In AD 597, Augustine landed in Kent, and the conversion of southern England began. It was only in England that Christianity had been submerged by *pagan* invaders.

In Italy, France and Spain all the invaders had been Christians of a sort. The Christianity of the Roman Empire survived, ensuring that Roman law and Latin languages continued.

POPE GREGORY One man played an enormous part in this: Pope Gregory, who sent Augustine to England in AD 597. His efforts had also led to the conversion of the Visigoths in Spain from *Arian* to Catholic ways. He was a great supporter of the monks and monasteries. Their importance for the next 1000 years as centers of learning and culture is due largely to him.

Key Dates in the Spread of Christianity

AD 590–604	Gregory the Great, Pope
AD 590–615	St Columban teaching in Lombardy and Burgundy
AD 597	Benedictine monks from Rome begin mission in Kent under St Augustine of Canterbury
AD 632	Conversion of East Anglia in England begins
AD 663/664	Synod of Whitby resolves differences between English and Celtic Christianity. Roman obedience confirmed
AD 680s	St Willibrod converts the Frisians of Holland
AD 719–741	St Boniface sent from England to convert. Germans
AD 754	Martyrdom of St Boniface
AD 860–5	Methodius converts the Bulgarians
AD 967	Christianity introduced in Poland
AD 988/989	Beginning of conversion of Russia to Christianity
AD 995–1000	Olaf Trygvasson introduces Christianity into Norway
AD 1076	Synod of Worms: bishops depose Pope Gregory. Beginning of a power struggle between the Popes and the Holy Roman Emperor

The spread of Christianity was fueled from three centers: the Celts in Ireland, the Roman Catholics in Rome, and the Eastern Orthodox Christians in Constantinople. Between them, they managed to spread Christianity through practically the whole of Europe.

Areas of Catholic Christianity

Areas of Eastern Christianity

Areas of Irish Christianity

Key missionary routes

Christianity in Europe

BERGEN

SCANDINAVIA

BALTIC SEA

POLAND

BRITAIN

LONDON

BLACK SEA

ATLANTIC OCEAN

FRANCE

CONSTANTINOPLE

TURKEY

ROME

ITALY

MEDITERRANEAN SEA

THE MISSIONARIES To the Catholic Church, the conversion of the *heathen* was a high priority. After the Arian *heretics* had been won over, the next targets were the tribes outside the old Roman frontiers. The monks went out on dangerous missions. St Gall, an Irishman, was one of the first, and with Frankish monks he founded monasteries in Bavaria, in south Germany.

In the AD 680s an English monk, Willibrod, converted the Frisians of Holland. It was one of his followers, Boniface, who was the most famous monk of all. From AD 719 to 741 he travelled through Germany, baptizing pagans by the thousands, closing their shrines and felling their sacred trees. He brought his new converts into the Catholic Church, recognizing the Pope as its head. It was because of men like Boniface and Gregory that the power of the Popes took hold. From then on the Pope was to be the spiritual leader of the western world.

THE EASTERN CHURCH Constantinople sent out its missionaries too, into Asia and eastern Europe. Most famous were Cyril and his brother Methodius, who converted the Bulgarians in AD 860-5. The Bulgarians were an illiterate tribe as savage as Attila's Huns. As well as religion, Cyril gave them letters, the *Cyrillic alphabet*, which is still used in Bulgaria and Russia today.

BEYOND CONSTANTINOPLE In the world even further east, in the centuries after Christ's crucifixion, Christianity had spread south and east. In Egypt the *Coptic* church ruled, and further south the kingdom of Ethiopia was Christian too. From Syria to Persia, and even further afield, almost as far as Mongolia, there were *Nestorian* Christians. These were followers of Nestorius, who had been expelled from Constantinople as a heretic. They survived in the depths of Asia for many centuries, living in peace with Muslims and *Buddhists*.

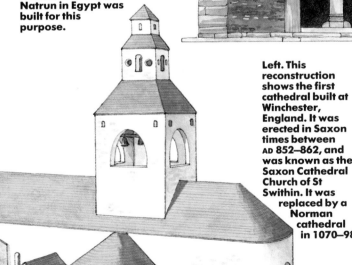

Above. To the early Christians, conversion of the 'heathens' was a high priority. First they would send missionaries out to convert the people, then they would construct lasting structures to make sure that Christianity endured. This monastery of St Bishoi in Al Wadi El Natrun in Egypt was built for this purpose.

Left. This reconstruction shows the first cathedral built at Winchester, England. It was erected in Saxon times between AD 852–862, and was known as the Saxon Cathedral Church of St Swithin. It was replaced by a Norman cathedral in 1070–98.

Above. This timber and drystone-walled Christian church at Debre Damo in Ethiopia was built in the fifth century AD. One of the Syrian saints suppressed a snake cult to found a monastery which adjoined the church. Debre Damo became a great center for Christian learning in Africa until its influence diminished in the thirteenth century.

CHARLEMAGNE AND THE FRANKS

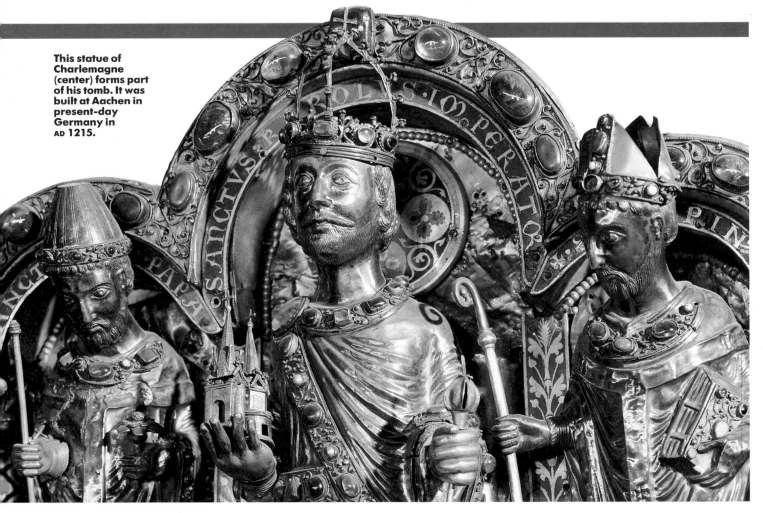

This statue of Charlemagne (center) forms part of his tomb. It was built at Aachen in present-day Germany in AD 1215.

At the beginning of the eighth century AD, the European kingdoms looked secure: 100 years later, everything had changed. In AD 711 an Islamic army of *Moors* (the tribes of North Africa) and Arabs arose. By AD 720 they had completely overrun the Visigothic kingdom and looked set to sweep north.

At the same time, Charles, ruler of the Franks, was expanding his power to the south. In AD 732 Abd-ar-Rahman, the governor of Spain, and Charles clashed at Tours in the south of France. The Moors were defeated and the governor killed. Their advance had been stopped and Charles was given the nickname 'Martel'–Charles the Hammer.

FRANKS AND ROME Charles' son, Pepin the Short (AD 751-768), pushed on again. The Pope, ruler of the city of Rome as well as the head of the Church, was under attack from the Lombards, a Germanic people who held the north of Italy. In 755 Pepin moved in, rescued the Pope and Rome, and established a special relationship between Rome and the Franks. Next he turned on the south of France and soon his realm, Francia, covered all of what is now France.

In AD 768 the crown passed to his son, Charles. Again there was trouble with the Lombards, and Charles marched across the Alps into Italy in AD 774. His victory made him King of the Franks and Lombards and, effectively, ruler of Rome.

A NEW EMPIRE Charles continued his conquests, but combined them with a sort of rough missionary work. In north Germany were the old Saxons, part of the tribe that had not gone to Britain. They were conquered and converted. In the south he took the northern part of Spain from the Moors, but not before Roland, one of his commanders, was killed at Roncevalles in the Pyrenees. This event soon become the favorite subject for songs and poems.

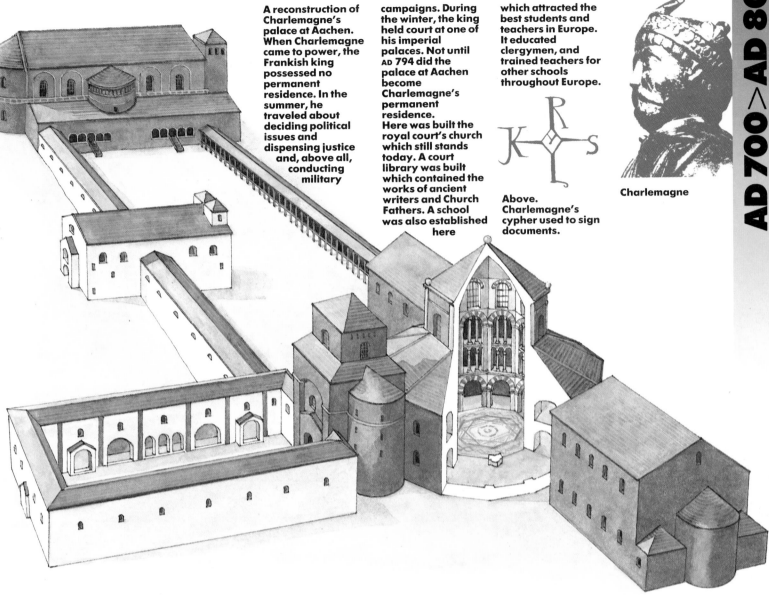

A reconstruction of Charlemagne's palace at Aachen. When Charlemagne came to power, the Frankish king possessed no permanent residence. In the summer, he traveled about deciding political issues and dispensing justice and, above all, conducting military campaigns. During the winter, the king held court at one of his imperial palaces. Not until AD 794 did the palace at Aachen become Charlemagne's permanent residence. Here was built the royal court's church which still stands today. A court library was built which contained the works of ancient writers and Church Fathers. A school was also established here which attracted the best students and teachers in Europe. It educated clergymen, and trained teachers for other schools throughout Europe.

Above. Charlemagne's cypher used to sign documents.

Charlemagne

Feudalism

KING   BISHOP   DUKE   COUNT

In Charlemagne's time, almost all people made their living by farming. Few people had much money and the government and laws of the old Roman Empire had disappeared.

Charlemagne improved conditions by granting large estates to loyal nobles, such as dukes and counts who, in return, provided military and political services to the king.

These nobles employed ordinary people to work on their land.

Members of the church also became important members of the community.

This arrangement, called *Feudalism*, became the basic political and military system of Europe for the next 400 years.

By AD 800 Charles ruled France, the west of Germany, and the north of Italy. On Christmas day, in St Peter's Church in Rome, Pope Leo III placed a crown on his head and declared him 'the great and peace-bringing Emperor of the Romans.' Charles of Francia had become 'Charlemagne,' Charles the Great, Holy Roman Emperor.

THE REIGN OF CHARLEMAGNE Under Charlemagne the Franks dominated the west of Europe. He was a great supporter of the church and he used it to encourage learning and culture. His court, traveling through the kingdom from one palace to the next, contained learned monks, like the English monk, Alcuin, and the Visigothic poet, Theodulf. Charlemagne himself could not write, yet he could understand Greek and Latin. He had the unwritten laws of his subjects collected and written. What the Roman emperors had done almost 1000 years before, he did again for his new empire.

THE VIKINGS: AT HOME AND ABROAD

Some 500 years after the Anglo-Saxons had descended on the old Roman Empire, more men of the north attacked the new Holy Roman Empire. They were *pagans*, looting and destroying Christian lands. History was repeating itself.

RAIDERS BY SEA This time they came from Norway and Denmark–the Norsemen, or Vikings. The popular picture of a Viking, a savage in a horned helmet, bent on total destruction, is picturesque, but wrong. Horned helmets had gone out of fashion 2000 years before. And although they were pirates and raiders, they were no different in this from most of the other peoples of their day. They were just better at it.

At home they were farmers and herdsmen, scratching a living from the poor land of Scandinavia. In the summers they became warriors and seamen, the most adventurous of the day.

Their longships are legendary, but we know more about them than legend: some have been preserved for more than 1000 years. One of the best known is a great ship buried in a grave at Gokstad in Norway. It was 26 yards long with a mast for the great red and white sail, and 34 oars.

THE GREAT JOURNEYS In 1893 a replica of this great ship was built, and in 28 days it safely sailed from Bergen in Norway to Newfoundland in Canada. This voyage was undertaken to prove that the legends of Viking voyages to America are more than myth.

About AD 870 they settled in Iceland, then an island almost deserted apart from a few Irish monks. In AD 982 Eirik the Red, an outlaw, settled in Greenland, cold and forbidding, but not so different from his homeland. Nineteen years later his son, Leif Eiriksson, took the next step and landed in Newfoundland. Eiriksson called this land Vinland. A present-day site at L'Anse aux Meadows is probably one of his winter camps. But there was no permanent settlement in America at this time.

VIKINGS IN THE EAST Swedish Vikings tended to travel east of their homeland. They traded first in the Baltic Sea for fur, slaves, timber and honey, and finally travelled up the great rivers of Poland and Russia. Many of them settled in towns like Novgorod and Kiev, where they were known as *Rus*. It was these Vikings who gave their name to the whole country, Russia. From here, they dragged their ships overland and sailed down the southward-flowing rivers into the Black Sea and Caspian Sea, trading and raiding as they went.

But they found other work too. Their fighting skills were well known to the eastern empire and to the Islamic world, and they were taken on as *mercenaries* there. The emperor in Constantinople was protected by the Varangian Guard, made up entirely of Vikings. Whether it was raiding, trading or soldiering, the Vikings were never slow to take their opportunities.

The Gods of the Vikings

The Vikings believed that the world was ruled by gods who lived in a heavenly place called *Asgard*. The greatest of their gods was Odin. He was the god most respected by Viking warriors, as they believed that he could give them courage, victory and wisdom.

The red-bearded Thor was the god of wind, rain and farming. Vikings believed that when he rode across the sky in

A ninth century AD stone head of Thor.

his chariot drawn by goats, there was thunder and lightning. He carried a huge stone hammer, called 'Mjollnir', which legend tells us he hurled at giants and trolls.

Frey was the god of marriage and growing things. When Vikings sowed their crops, they scattered bread and poured wine or beer on the ground. This was done to please Frey who would then make the crops grow tall and strong.

Odin is shown above on an 8-legged horse. The soapstone below features the face of Loki, a god associated with destruction.

A ninth century AD stone head of Frey.

34

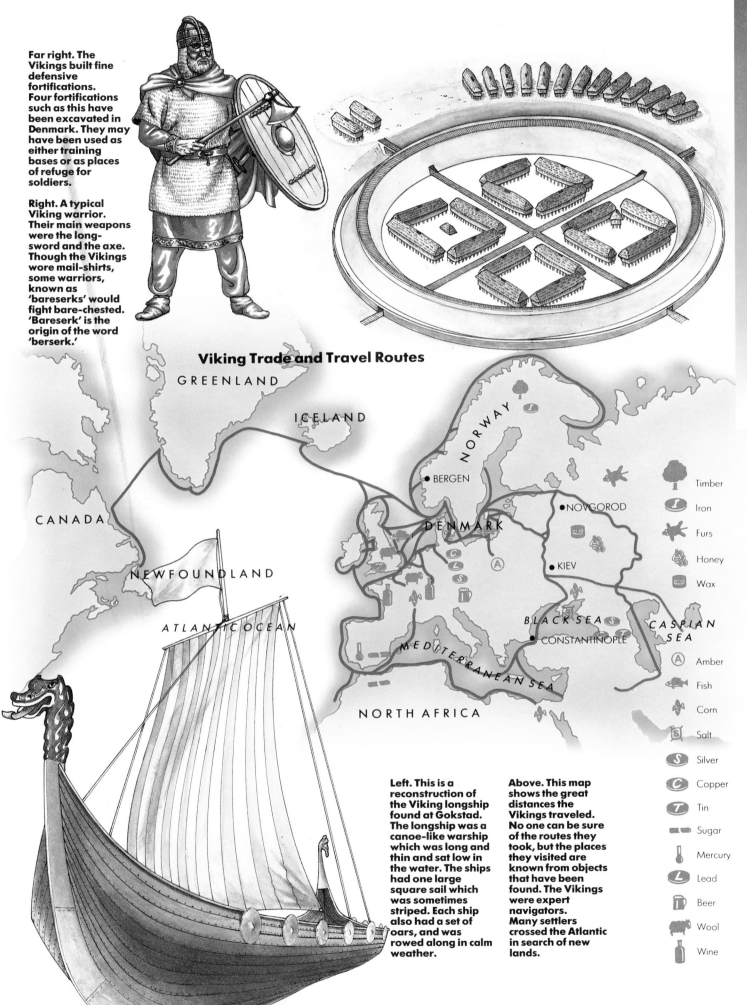

Far right. The Vikings built fine defensive fortifications. Four fortifications such as this have been excavated in Denmark. They may have been used as either training bases or as places of refuge for soldiers.

Right. A typical Viking warrior. Their main weapons were the long-sword and the axe. Though the Vikings wore mail-shirts, some warriors, known as 'bareserks' would fight bare-chested. 'Bareserk' is the origin of the word 'berserk.'

Viking Trade and Travel Routes

GREENLAND

ICELAND

NORWAY

BERGEN

CANADA

DENMARK

NOVGOROD

KIEV

NEWFOUNDLAND

ATLANTIC OCEAN

BLACK SEA

CASPIAN SEA

CONSTANTINOPLE

MEDITERRANEAN SEA

NORTH AFRICA

Timber
Iron
Furs
Honey
Wax
Amber
Fish
Corn
Salt
Silver
Copper
Tin
Sugar
Mercury
Lead
Beer
Wool
Wine

Left. This is a reconstruction of the Viking longship found at Gokstad. The longship was a canoe-like warship which was long and thin and sat low in the water. The ships had one large square sail which was sometimes striped. Each ship also had a set of oars, and was rowed along in calm weather.

Above. This map shows the great distances the Vikings traveled. No one can be sure of the routes they took, but the places they visited are known from objects that have been found. The Vikings were expert navigators. Many settlers crossed the Atlantic in search of new lands.

THE VIKINGS: CONQUERORS AND SETTLERS

In western Europe, the Vikings were adaptable. In the Shetlands, Orkney and the Hebrides, where there was land to be had, they settled as farmers, with piracy as a side interest, in about AD 780. Further south, where the land was richer and already densely settled, they had to take another approach–full scale invasion.

THE SCALE OF THE VIKING INVASION About AD 840 Norwegian Vikings invaded Ireland. They set up trading towns in Dublin, Waterford, Wexford, Limerick and Cork. Here, in wooden houses by the riverside ports, they traded with the Irish and the rest of Europe and went raiding from time to time.

Meanwhile the Danish Vikings were loose in the North Sea and the English Channel. In AD 793 they had pillaged the monastery of Lindisfarne, an act which shocked Christian England. Holland, Belgium and France were their prey too, and great ports like London, Dorestadt and Quentovic were destroyed. Further south they were less lucky. The *Moors* of Spain were better prepared, and in AD 844 Viking corpses hung from the palm trees of Seville and Viking heads were sent as presents to Africa.

THE INVASION OF ENGLAND In AD 862 Danish raids on England turned to invasion. The east and north of England became *Danelaw*, the Danish kingdom, but in the south, Alfred, King of Wessex, held out and pushed them back. By AD 924 much of England was English again. It was around York that the Viking power lasted longest. Here the Norsemen had a settlement like the ones in Ireland, and archaeology has turned up the smallest details of their lives.

In AD 994 the Danes were back. From fortified camps, like Trelleborg in Denmark, the armies of Svein Forkbeard and his Norwegian ally Olaf Tryggvason attacked. Only blackmail payments of mountains of silver by King Ethelred held them off. Finally Cnut (Canute) became King of England and Denmark, and the two kingdoms were one for 26 years.

NORMAN NORSEMEN The coast of France was suffering too. But in AD 911 the King of the Franks set a thief to catch thieves, and gave part of his kingdom to Rollo and his Viking band. They wanted land and the Franks wanted protection from other Vikings; it was a fair bargain. In a few years this part of France took the Norsemen's name and became Normandy. Their war leader became the Duke of Normandy and they became Christians.

As fighting men they were in demand, and they were invited to Italy in 1016 to help settle local wars. They fought and they stayed, setting themselves up in a Norman kingdom that covered southern Italy.

Fifty years later, Duke William of Normandy launched the last great Viking raid. In 1066 his army crossed the Channel to England. At the Battle of Hastings they defeated the English and William became the king of England. Alcuin wrote in AD 793.

Never before has such terror appeared in Britain as we have now suffered from a pagan race, nor was it thought that such an inroad from the sea could be made. Behold the church of St Cuthbert, spattered with the blood of the priests of God, despoiled of all its ornaments; a place more venerable than all in Britain is given as a prey to pagan peoples.

Left. This Viking spear is made of bronze and has a highly decorated hilt. Though not known particularly for their arts and crafts, the Vikings have left behind some beautiful artifacts. Fine weapons were greatly prized among Vikings, and were handed down from father to son.

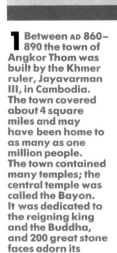

Right. Contrary to popular images of Vikings in horned helmets, this carved head shows the typical plain, conical helmets that were generally worn.

Below. This is a reconstruction of what a typical Viking town probably looked like. Many of the streets would have been paved with logs. Houses varied in size and most would have had several storage huts or work places. These would all have been enclosed by a wooden fence.

The Runic Alphabet

ᚠᚢᛒ ᛞᛟᛗᛖᚠᚾᛁᛋ

ᛗᛁᛟᚲᚱᛦᛖᛏᚺᛈ

The Vikings used the Runic script. The origin of the Runic alphabet is uncertain, but probably dates from the first century BC or AD.

It is more than likely that runes had solely a monumental use. There is no certain evidence that they were ever used in a literary way–to record stories, legends or poems.

Three main varieties of the alphabet can be found on the 4000 inscriptions which have been found. The 'Old Teutonic' consisted of 24 letters. The Anglican *Futhark*, brought to Britain in the fifth and sixth centuries AD, increased the letters to 28. The alphabet was increased again to 33 letters in the ninth century AD, as the 'Old Teutonic' letters were not sufficient to represent all the old English sounds.

1 Between AD 860–890 the town of Angkor Thom was built by the Khmer ruler, Jayavarman III, in Cambodia. The town covered about 4 square miles and may have been home to as many as one million people. The town contained many temples; the central temple was called the Bayon. It was dedicated to the reigning king and the Buddha, and 200 great stone faces adorn its towers.

2 On 25 December AD 800, Charles, King of the Franks and Lombards, was pronounced Emperor of the Holy Roman Empire. This marked the first time since the fall of the Roman Empire that a ruler had emerged who was strong enough to unify western Europe. His imperial coronation was an important sign that, after 400 years of invasions and chaos, Europe was on its way to recovery.

ARTS AND CRAFTS OF THE DARK AGES

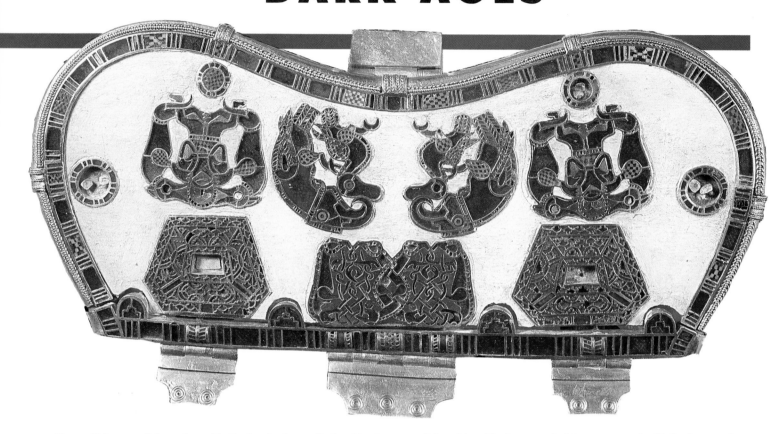

Above. This purse lid was found in the Anglo-Saxon Sutton Hoo treasure. It is gold and is decorated with garnets and millefiori enamels.
Below. This silver brooch is typical of the intricate and fine work that Viking craftsmen produced.

From Scandinavia to Spain and from Britain to Bulgaria, the people of the Dark Ages all had their own artistic styles, ways of building and handicrafts. But they were all very different from the Roman ways that had gone before and which survived in the East.

MATERIALS IN USE Gold, enamel (a sort of colored glass) and jewels were used lavishly on the most important objects. The art of the Anglo-Saxons, the Lombards and the Vikings is alive with squirming interlacing animals, in gilded bronze, gold, ivory or wood. On the other hand, the Franks, Visigoths and Vandals favored gaudier colors and their art glows with red and green jewels and enamel on gold backgrounds.

Whatever was important at the time was lavishly decorated. Anglo-Saxon pottery urns to contain the ashes of the dead have extravagant curving or stamped decoration. The hilts of the swords were alive with gilded twisting animals twined around each other.

When Christianity took hold, time and attention were lavished on Bibles and on reliquaries–boxes to hold the sacred *relics* of the saints.

Above. This beautiful gold and enamel jewel is generally thought to have been owned by Alfred the Great, a British Saxon

King. A Saxon inscription around the jewel reads 'Aelfred mec heht gewyrcan' which means 'Alfred had me made'.

Above. This page from the *Lindisfarne Gospel* shows how fine the work was of the monks who toiled over these beautiful hand-made books during the Dark Ages. Many manuscripts were beautifully decorated in bright colors—often gold or silver leaf was used on the initial letters and the decoration. Such manuscripts were called 'illuminated' because they looked as if they were lit from inside.

Below. This Merovingian brooch dates from the seventh/eighth centuries AD. It is typical of the art of

the European settlers who used bright jewels and enamels to decorate their jewelry.

Europe in Confusion
TIME CHART

AD	THE MEDITERRANEAN	NORTHERN EUROPE
200		Barbarian invasions begin
285	Administrative separation of the eastern and western halves of the Roman Empire	
330	Foundation of Constantinople	
378	Battle of Adrianople	Angles and Saxons raid Britain
408		The Romans leave Britain
410	Visigoths capture Rome. This leads to the collapse of the Western Roman Empire	St Patrick converts Ireland to Christianity Angles and Saxons settle in Britain
452	Attila and the Huns in Italy	
476	Last Roman Emperor deposed	
500		Villages of northern Europe abandoned due to flooding. Germanic peoples migrate eastwards and southwards
530	Byzantines invade Italy	
532	Haghia Sophia, the great domed cathedral of Constantinople, built by Justinian	
542		Bubonic plague in Europe
590	Gregory I, 'The Great,' becomes Pope	
597		St Augustine in England
610	The Eastern Roman Emperor, Heraclius, Hellenizes the Empire. From now on it is known as the Byzantine Empire	
625		Sutton Hoo burial in Suffolk, England, contains grave goods from Sweden, France and Constantinople
700		Willibrod and Boniface preach in Germany
711	Arabs invade Spain	
732		Charles Martel halts the Arab advance into Europe
751	Ravenna captured by the Lombards	
762	Abbasid capital of Baghdad founded	
800	Charlemagne becomes Holy Roman Emperor	Viking raids begin
843	Treaty of Verdun divides Holy Roman Empire into three parts	
870		Vikings in Iceland
882		Vikings set up a state in Russia, centred in Kiev
969	Fatimids conquer Egypt and found Cairo	
982		Eirik the Red settles in Greenland
1001		Leif Eiriksson travels to America

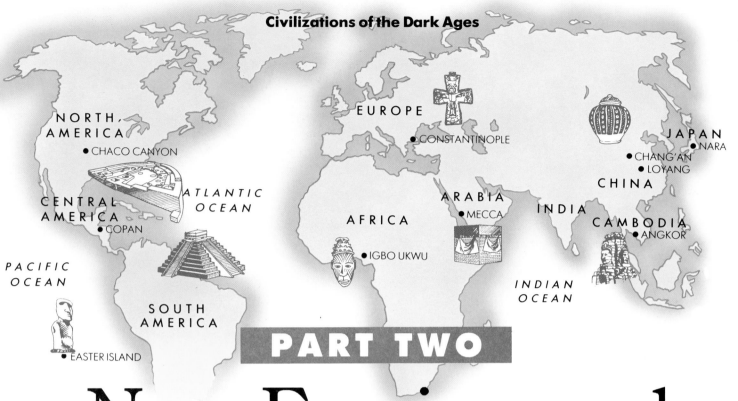

PART TWO

New Empires and Cultures

While Europe was in its 'Dark Ages', what was happening in the rest of the world? It was faring much better. In what had been the eastern part of the Roman Empire, the Byzantines ruled an empire, part-Roman and part-Greek, from Turkey to Egypt, where much of the learning of the Greeks and Romans was kept alive. But enemies were pressing in on the Byzantines all the time–first the Persians and then the Islamic Empire.

THE BIRTH OF ISLAM The founding of the religion of Islam was perhaps the most important event that happened in this period. Three of the world's great faiths had already been founded–Hinduism, Buddhism and Christianity. The fourth, *Islam*, now appeared.

In the twentieth century we all know how much power Islam wields, and how dedicated its followers are. At the beginning it was the same, or even more so. In less than 150 years Islam had spread all over the Middle East, through Persia to India in the east, and in the west along the north coast of Africa into Spain. Here Islamic Arabs, or *Moors*, were to rule until the Middle Ages. What sort of religion was it that inspired such conquests? Was it just a military machine? What was the cultural and

intellectual life of Islam like? All these questions will be answered in the following pages.

EASTERN EMPIRES India and China suffered barbarian invasions like Europe, but managed to absorb them. They continued to develop glorious cultures and civilizations, spreading their own influence into Korea, Japan and Southeast Asia.

Trade flourished in this period, both by sea, from China to India and Arabia and so into Europe, and overland too. The great Silk Road, from China to the shores of the Mediterranean Sea, connected the west with the farthest countries of Asia, bringing silk, perfume and other luxury goods into Dark Age Europe.

NEW CULTURES Even further afield progress continued. Intrepid explorers from Southeast Asia made daring journeys into the unknown to settle the Polynesian islands of the Pacific Ocean. Rich civilizations and empires sprang up in Africa, and in America the huge temple-cities of the Olmecs and Maya, as ambitious and splendid as anything that Europe had ever produced, were being built in the jungle.

MEDITERRANEAN TRADE

The Roman Empire lived on its trade. Great cities like Rome, Carthage in North Africa, Alexandria in Egypt, Antioch in Syria and Constantinople at the crossroads of Europe and Asia, had been the centers of great networks. Goods flooded into them from inside and outside the Empire. They were bought, sold and shipped on. The end of the Roman Empire did not mean the end of the trade, but with so many kingdoms on the north side of the Mediterranean it became more complicated. Each one had its own rules and levied its own taxes, thus trade became more expensive.

ISLAMIC EMPIRE But after the seventh century AD the south side of the Mediterranean was held together by the Islamic Empire, which protected and promoted trade just as the Romans had done. Much of the trade here was in the hands of Jewish merchants, who could pass freely from one end of the empire to the other, always able to speak their own language to brother merchants, always sure of a friendly reception wherever they went.

THE NORTH AFRICAN ROUTE A new trade route grew up from Spain to Asia, along the north coast of Africa, and new cities like Tunis and Kairouan grew up to serve it. The sea was still the cheapest means of transport. A shipload of goods took 30 days to travel from Alexandria to Marseilles in France, but ships could only sail between April and October for fear of storms.

In North Africa, trade goods were mostly carried by camels. *Caravans* of camels had been crossing North Africa ever since the Roman period, and under the Arabs they carried wine, salt, oil and European goods eastward, and eastern luxuries westward.

These ancient *amphorae* were found in Turkey. Goods such as oil and wine would have been transported in amphorae like these throughout the Mediterranean.

THE NORTH European trade came into the system by several routes. Some from the North Sea area went to ports like London, Dorestad and Quentovic and then by sea to Spain. Another route led up the French rivers and overland to the Alps.

From the Alps, trade routes from all over Europe converged on Italy. At the head of the Adriatic Sea, a small city was beginning to build up a trading empire. This was Venice, and soon it had a firm grip on trade links with the Islamic world. Frankish swords, furs, tin, lead, wax, honey and timber were all shipped south out of Venice. But one other trade was even more important– the slave trade to Byzantium and the cities of the East. Many of these slaves were Slavs from eastern Europe who were often prisoners of war. The word 'slave' is derived from the word 'Slav'—which shows how many Slavs must have been bought and sold.

The trade from Venice connected into the main east-west trade route. The details had changed since the Roman period, but the Mediterranean market still thrived and lived on.

Though this is a modern-day caravan, carrying salt from Niger in Africa, the caravans transporting goods in the Dark Ages period probably looked little different.

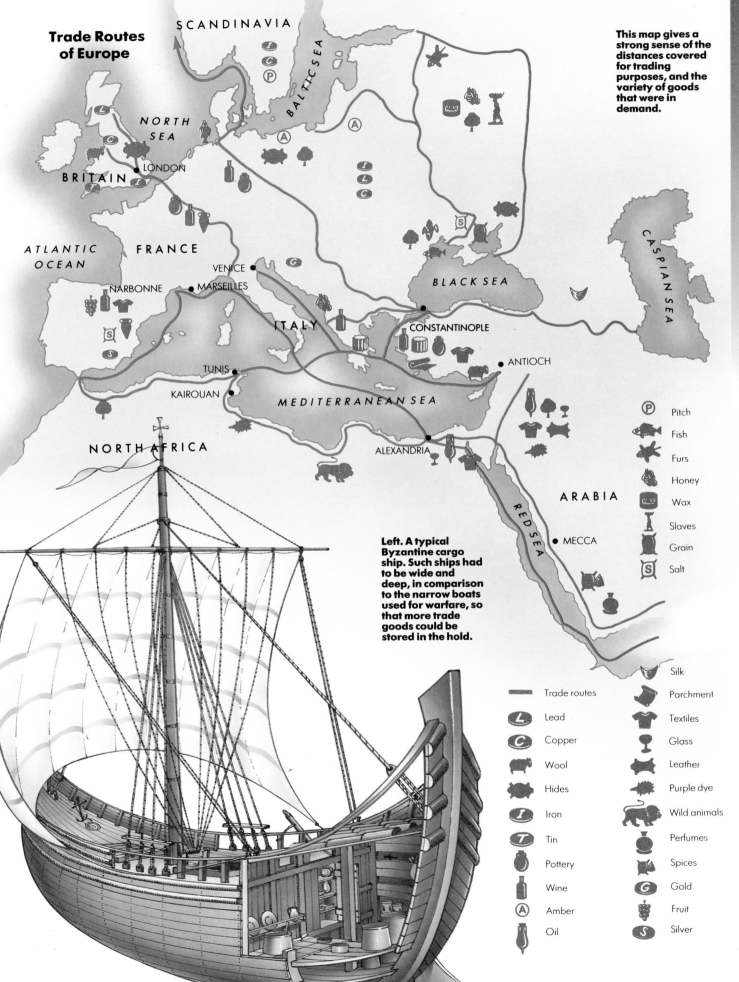

Trade Routes of Europe

Trade Routes
of Europe

This map gives a
strong sense of the
distances covered
for trading
purposes, and the
variety of goods
that were in
demand.

SCANDINAVIA

BALTIC SEA

NORTH
SEA

BRITAIN

LONDON

ATLANTIC
OCEAN

FRANCE

VENICE

NARBONNE

MARSEILLES

ITALY

CASPIAN SEA

BLACK SEA

CONSTANTINOPLE

ANTIOCH

TUNIS

KAIROUAN

MEDITERRANEAN SEA

ALEXANDRIA

NORTH AFRICA

ARABIA

RED SEA

MECCA

Left. A typical
Byzantine cargo
ship. Such ships had
to be wide and
deep, in comparison
to the narrow boats
used for warfare, so
that more trade
goods could be
stored in the hold.

Symbol	Good
(P)	Pitch
	Fish
	Furs
	Honey
	Wax
	Slaves
	Grain
(S)	Salt
	Silk
	Parchment
	Textiles
	Glass
	Leather
	Purple dye
	Wild animals
	Perfumes
	Spices
(G)	Gold
	Fruit
(S)	Silver

Symbol	Good
——	Trade routes
(L)	Lead
(C)	Copper
	Wool
	Hides
(I)	Iron
(T)	Tin
	Pottery
	Wine
(A)	Amber
	Oil

43

FROM CONSTANTINOPLE TO BYZANTIUM

This thirteenth century Greek manuscript shows the Byzantines using the chemical weapon known as *Greek Fire* against the Arabs.

While the Western Roman Empire was changing into the new kingdoms of Europe, life in the east was very different.

ROMAN OR GREEK In the fifth century AD, Constantinople ruled an empire of Greece, Yugoslavia, Romania, Bulgaria, Turkey, Syria, Israel, Egypt and Lybia. Even in the heyday of Rome these countries had been as much Greek as Roman, and in a century or so after the decline of the Roman Empire, there was little Roman about them at all. To outsiders the empire of Constantinople was peopled by 'Greeks'. We refer to the empire as 'Byzantine,' after the name of the original Greek city, Byzantium, which the Roman Emperor Constantine had rebuilt and renamed after himself–Constantinople.

THE EMPIRE LIVES ON The Byzantine Empire lasted a thousand years longer than the Roman one, until AD 1453. How was this achieved? It was attacked from the outside many times. In AD 441 and AD 447 Huns plundered the whole of Greece; in the AD 460s and AD 470s the Ostrogoths were as much of a threat. Even when Zeno, the Byzantine Emperor, distracted the Huns by sending them to attack Italy in his name, and so took the pressure off Byzantium, the Avars and the Bulgars replaced them and menaced the Byzantine Empire for centuries after.

PERSIANS AND ARABS In the east the great threat was Persia. Warfare between the Persians and Byzantines across the deserts of Syria and Iraq lasted, on and off, until Persia was conquered by the Arabs in AD 650. At the same time, the Arabs took Lybia, Syria and Israel from the Byzantines. Even worse than this, the Arabs took control of Egypt, where most of the food supplies of Constantinople came from.

So great were the Empire's losses that by AD 700 it was only a shadow of what it had formerly been, covering little more territory than Turkey and Greece. But still it survived.

THE BYZANTINE NAVY Part of the reason for its survival was its sea power. The Byzantine navy was the most powerful of its day, and was equipped with a horrific chemical weapon known as *Greek Fire*. This was a mixture of pitch, naphtha and sulphur which could be shot, like a flame thrower, at enemy fleets. It could just as easily be packed into pottery bombs–the earliest form of hand grenades.

THE WALLS OF CONSTANTINOPLE The city of Constantinople was magnificently defended: even when enemies conquered Greece or Turkey, the city remained intact behind its immense walls, resisting attack like a rock in the ocean. In AD 626 it held out against a combined attack by Avars from Greece, and Arabs who had invaded Turkey.

Every year from AD 674 to AD 677 it was attacked and besieged by Arabs, and one siege lasted more than a year. But still the city survived, defended by its fleet and by its army, many of whom were *Varangians*–Vikings from Scandinavia and Russia. For the last few centuries the Byzantine Empire steadily shrank, but from time to time a warrior-emperor like Basil II would arise and reconquer some of its old land.

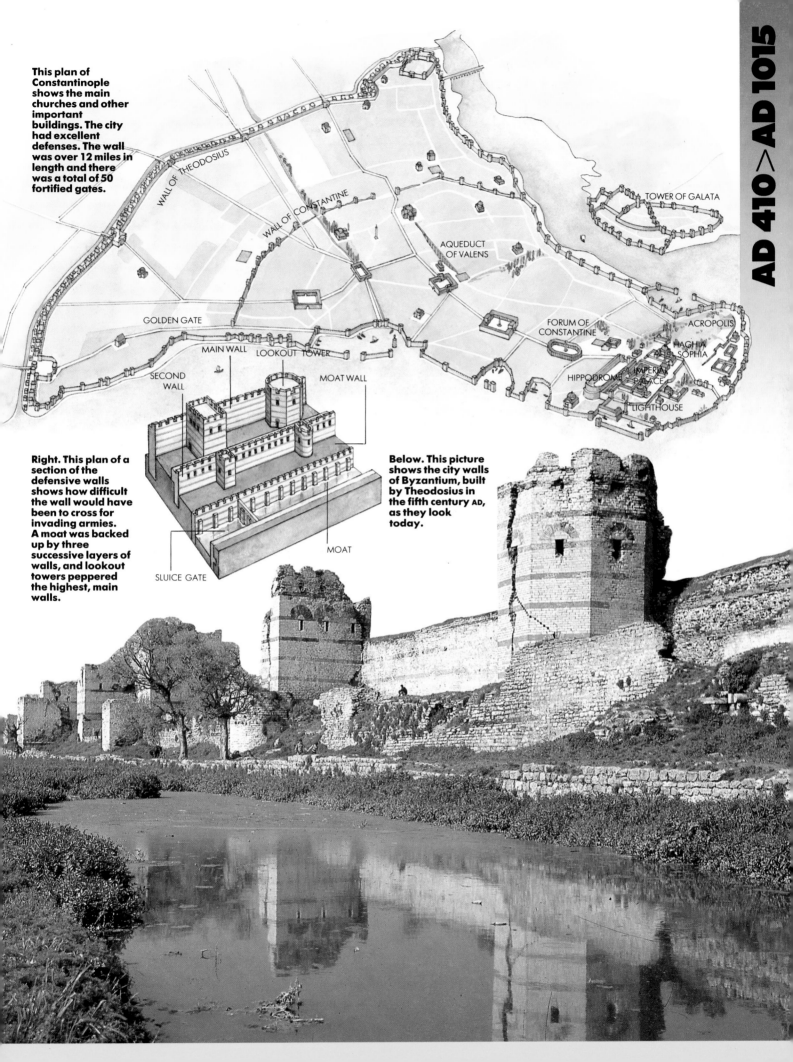

This plan of Constantinople shows the main churches and other important buildings. The city had excellent defenses. The wall was over 12 miles in length and there was a total of 50 fortified gates.

WALL OF THEODOSIUS

WALL OF CONSTANTINE

TOWER OF GALATA

AQUEDUCT OF VALENS

GOLDEN GATE

FORUM OF CONSTANTINE

ACROPOLIS

HAGHIA SOPHIA

HIPPODROME

IMPERIAL PALACE

LIGHTHOUSE

MAIN WALL

LOOKOUT TOWER

MOAT WALL

SECOND WALL

MOAT

SLUICE GATE

Right. This plan of a section of the defensive walls shows how difficult the wall would have been to cross for invading armies. A moat was backed up by three successive layers of walls, and lookout towers peppered the highest, main walls.

Below. This picture shows the city walls of Byzantium, built by Theodosius in the fifth century AD, as they look today.

BYZANTINE ART AND CULTURE

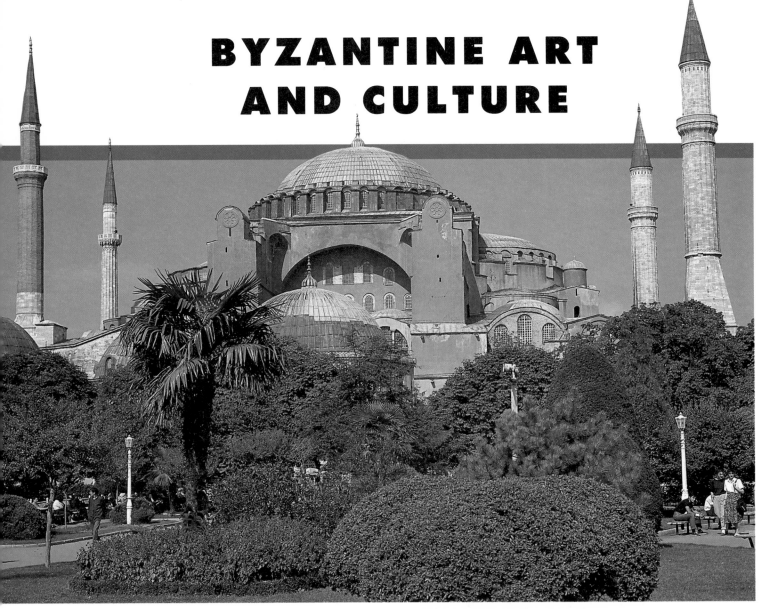

When we look at what the Byzantines left behind them, it is easy to see what they thought was important. Their art and their buildings tell us a great deal.

LIVING ON THE LAND Outside the great cities, the Byzantines were farmers, like the Romans before them. Peasants grew corn, grapes and olives, and looked after flocks of sheep and goats. Rich landowners adorned with gold jewelry, toured their estates supervising the work, and lived in luxury.

IMPERIAL MAJESTY At the center of the Byzantine world was the Emperor: his face and figure were shown in art and on coins in the way that he wanted it to be seen. So the Emperor Anastasius, shown on an ivory panel as a young soldier receiving ambassadors from India, was actually about 70 at the time that the panel was created. It was important in the Byzantine world to create an image of power and youthfulness.

Above. The Church of Haghia Sophia at Istanbul (Constantinople) as it appears today. The Emperor Justinian began its construction in AD 532. The church towered over all other buildings in the city. Its interior measures 100 yards wide and 200 yards high, and, when built, was the largest of any church in Europe.

Left. This Byzantine ivory *diptych* depicts men fighting bears at the games, watched by the court. It dates from the fifth century AD.

The Art of Mosaic

Above. This is a detail of the mosaic shown opposite, enlarged. You can see the great skill that is involved in creating mosaics.

Mosaics were first used for decoration by the Ancient Greeks, but it was the Romans who developed the art of mosaic extensively.

Influenced by Roman art forms, the Byzantines went on to create some of the finest mosaics ever produced.

Mosaics of religious scenes were used to decorate the walls and ceilings of many Byzantine churches. Craftsmen used *tesserae* (the pieces from which the mosaic was formed) of gold, silver, glass, stone and terracotta to produce some breathtaking effects.

Above. A detail of a floor mosaic in the Great Palace at Istanbul, c. AD 565. Byzantine mosaics featured a wide variety of subject matter, from simple scenes such as this man feeding his donkey, to depictions of Jesus Christ.

Right. This ninth century AD cross is a very fine example of Byzantine craftsmanship in enamel.

CHRISTIAN GLORY The splendor of the emperors was matched by the glory of the Church. Monasteries and churches of the Byzantine Empire, which we would now call Greek Orthodox, were beautiful places. Where the treasures and furnishings have survived years of looting by Turks, Vikings and other Christians, they are astonishingly rich. The Church of Haghia Sophia marked a pinnacle of Byzantine architecture. This beautiful building towered over the city at the height of the Empire and was the largest of any church in Europe.

Byzantine ideas rubbed off onto neighboring lands, too. Barbarian tribes like Slavs, Bulgars and Avars who attacked or traded with the Byzantines borrowed much from them, including their language, writing and art. The new barbarian art was often as beautiful as anything that the Empire itself could produce.

JUSTINIAN AND THEODORA

Of all the characters of the Byzantine Empire, the most colorful are the Emperor Justinian and his Empress Theodora. In their reign the empire reached its greatest extent and saw its most stirring times.

PEASANT EMPERORS Justinian's uncle, Justin, a peasant from Bulgaria who had made his name as a soldier, was made emperor by the army in AD 518. Because he was uneducated and illiterate, his nephew acted as the power behind the throne. When Justin died, Justinian replaced him as Emperor with his wife becoming Empress.

Theodora was ambitious and determined to wield power in the Empire. The portraits of these two characters, in the mosaics of Ravenna, show them as imperial rulers, bedecked with finery.

RIOTS IN THE HIPPODROME The first crisis during their period of rule occurred in AD 532. Chariot racing in the *hippodrome* (the racecourse) was a national craze.

Above. This mosaic from the Basilica of San Vitale in Ravenna depicts the Emperor Justinian (crowned) and his court.
Left. The Empress Theodora from a mosaic accompanying the one above in the Basilica of San Vitale. Both mosaics date from the sixth century AD.

At its height, the Byzantine Empire covered a huge area. In its extent it rivalled the Roman Empire which had dominated the Mediterranean world four centuries earlier.

The Byzantine Empire

▢ Maximum extent of the Empire

The Basilica of San Vitale in Ravenna, Italy. It is here where the mosaics of Justinian and Theodora shown opposite can be seen today. This Basilica houses some of the finest mosaics of the Byzantine period.

Key Dates of the Byzantine Empire

AD 500–642	Constant fighting between Persia and Byzantium
AD 527–565	Justinian, Emperor of Byzantium. He was responsible for modifying Byzantine laws
AD 534	Belisarius conquers the Vandals of North Africa
AD 535–554	Byzantium reconquers Italy
AD 542–546	Plague spreads in Byzantine Empire
AD 565–578	Justin II, Emperor of Byzantium
AD 572–628	Persians control Arabia
AD 626	Emperor Heraclius of Byzantium expels Persians from Egypt
AD 642	Final defeat of Persians by Arabs at Nehawand

The whole city was divided between the supporters of one team, the Blues, and the other, the Greens. Regularly the two groups of rival supporters came to blows, and the trouble had to be put down by force.

Unfortunately, Justinian went too far on this occasion, and found the two sides united against him. Blues and Greens together rampaged through the city and much of it was burned to the ground.

In the emergency, Justinian called on his best and most trusted general, Belisarius, who had just returned from fighting against Persia. He marched into the hippodrome and slaughtered 30,000 rioters, putting an end to the crisis.

VANDALS, GOTHS AND PERSIANS Justinian had one great ambition: to restore the old Roman Empire and to rule it. He sent an army, with the great general Belisarius to lead it, to start the reconquest in AD 533. First to fall were the Vandals of Tunisia in AD 534.

For the next 19 years Byzantium was at war. First, Belisarius fought his way up through Italy, taking control of Rome from the Ostrogoths in AD 536, and taking Ravenna, in northern Italy, in AD 540.

At this point Justinian recalled Belisarius for service on the eastern frontier, where a new Persian king, Chosroes, was destroying Byzantine cities and armies. Not even Belisarius could stop the Persian King; only bubonic plague in Persia, and huge payments of Roman gold brought his attacks to an end.

At the same time, Huns and Slavs were invading the Empire from the north; four times between AD 540 and AD 558 they were beaten back.

In AD 551, the Ostrogoths fought back in Italy to try to reestablish their control. This time Justinian sent his court chamberlain, an 80 year-old with little military experience, called Narses. Despite his age and lack of qualifications, the old man succeeded and secured Italy. He then went on, after taking Italy, to add part of Spain to the Byzantine Empire.

By the time Justinian died, in AD 565, he had rebuilt a huge empire, extending from Syria to Spain. This was the golden age of the Byzantine Empire.

THE BIRTH OF ISLAM

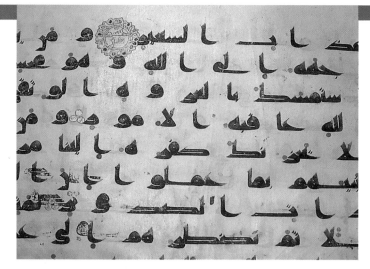

The Arabian Desert was the home of nomadic tribes with cities in the fertile oases. These cities had grown rich on the trade in spices and *frankincense*, and in AD 525 the kingdom of Axum sent its army across the Red Sea to conquer southern Arabia. Thirty-six years later, in the Year of the Elephant (AD 571), a great battle was fought near Mecca, and the combined Arab tribes defeated the Axumites.

THE HOLY CITY AND THE PROPHET Mecca was already sacred to the Arabs, who came as pilgrims to the Ka'ba, a shrine containing a sacred black stone. It was a center for the worship of the desert gods, a religion which had a lot in common with that of another desert people, the Jews.

In AD 610, there was a rich merchant of Mecca, named Muhammad. He was a deeply religious, mystical man, who believed that God had spoken to him with a new message: 'There is One God (Allah) and Muhammad is his *Prophet*.' He preached a new religion of obedience and equality, in which earlier prophets–Isaiah, Elijah, and Christ–all had a place. But his teachings, like those of other prophets before him, were revolutionary, and on 24 September, AD 622 he was forced to flee his home town to the nearby city of Medina.

THE BEGINNING OF ISLAM This flight, the *Hegira*, marks the beginning of Islam. At Medina, Muhammad

M uslims believe that the words of *Allah* were dictated to Mohammad by the angel Gabriel a little at a time. He learned them by heart, and repeated them to his followers. Some of them, who could write, took the words down 'on date leaves and pieces of white stone.' Others

The Qur'an

learned them by heart. Eventually they were collected into a single book, the *Qur'an*, which contains the central teachings of Islam.

The *Qur'an* is divided into chapters, called *suras*. The longest *suras* come first and contain

Above. This is a page from a ninth century AD *Qur'an*. It is written in an early Kufic script and is ornamented with gold.

instructions about how Muslims should carry out their daily life. The shortest *suras* at the end give warnings about the Day of Judgement.

Left. This beautiful Islamic tile shows the original Holy Mosque of the Prophet Mohammad at Medina. When Mohammad fled Mecca in AD 622 he went to Medina, where he set up the first Islamic government. This was the first Islamic mosque ever built, and a mosque of the same name still stands on the site today. The Mosque houses Mohammad's tomb, making Medina one of the most important centers of the Islamic faith. Because of this, pilgrims will generally also visit Medina when they make their pilgrimage to Mecca.

and his followers devised the laws of their new way of life. Soon, he was the ruler of Medina, and had created an Islamic society which combined strict religious rules with commandments to protect the weak–particularly women, slaves and orphans.

The Arabs were a warlike people, and it was natural that their new religion should be spread by war and conquest rather than by peaceful conversion. In AD 630 Muhammad captured Mecca and led 10,000 warriors into the city on *pilgrimage*. It now became the holy city of Islam, and the Ka'ba, the old pagan shrine, was its most sacred spot.

Muhammad, who had been a refugee, died in AD 632 as the ruler of most of Arabia.

He left behind the beginnings of a mighty empire, and something else even more important.

A NEW WAY OF LIFE The tribes of Arabia had been warlike and quarrelsome, with fierce loyalty to their families. Muhammad took this loyalty and turned it to himself and to the new religion, which has now spread all over the world. The western idea of Islam is often one of a conquering, warlike religion. But it was also a religion that allowed Jews, Christians and Buddhists to live in peace as respected citizens. Islam took the best of what it found and turned that into something very special. Muhammad is probably one of the most important men who ever lived.

Left. A reconstruction of how Mecca may have looked in the early years of Islam. The Ka'ba is the small square building in the center of the picture. Until AD 630 it housed the stones and other objects held sacred by the tribes of Arabia, in an inner chamber.

All except the sacred 'Black Stone' were removed by Mohammad in AD 630 when he retook the city of Mecca. At this point, the Ka'ba became the center of the Muslim world. Even today, Muslims must make a pilgrimage to Mecca at least once in their lifetimes.

THE HOLY WAR

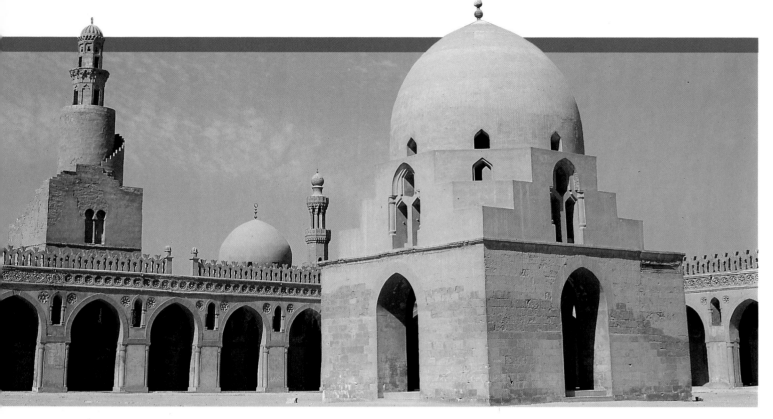

The conquests of Islam led to mosques being constructed in territory controlled by the Arabs. This mosque—the Ibn Tulun Mosque—was built in Cairo, Egypt, in the ninth century AD.

When Muhammad died in AD 632, one of his most loyal followers, Abu Bakr, was elected to follow him as *Caliph*, or representative. From now on Islamic rulers were given the title, *Caliph*, meaning the representative of Muhammad on earth. Until AD 655, former disciples of Muhammad ruled the Islamic lands from Medina, but then, after six years of civil war, the tribe of the Ummayads took control, and ruled the empire of Islam from their capital at Damascus in Syria.

THE CONQUESTS The Ummayads kept control until AD 749 when the Abbasids took over the empire. They ruled from a splendid new capital at Baghdad, in Iraq. In the 117 years since the death of Muhammad, an extraordinary thing had happened: Islam had grown from covering a small part of Arabia to ruling an immense empire which spread from the Atlantic Ocean to India.

The advance of the Arabs was even more devastating than the eruption of the Huns into the West. First they moved on the Byzantine Empire: by AD 642 they had conquered Syria and Egypt. Here, in trading cities like Alexandria, the Arabs acquired navies, and willing native peoples who were often pleased to be rid of the Byzantines.

AFRICA AND THE EAST The Byzantine Empire in Asia was now based mainly on Turkey, but even here the Arabs sometimes reached as far as Constantinople.

In the east, they swept through Persia and Asia. In AD 750 they defeated a Chinese army. In the other

Left. This fine example of Islamic craftsmanship in ivory depicts two men on horseback picking dates from a palm tree.

52

Right. Many of the first Muslim soldiers rode camels or horses. Their favored weapons were lances, swords, and bows and arrows. Shirts made of mail or of leather gave protection against enemy attack.

Arabs often defeated their enemies in battle by pretending to be beaten, and riding away. When the enemy chased after them, the Arabs would turn on them and make an unexpected and deadly attack.

1 By AD 700 three principal cultures had emerged in the southwestern region of North America: the Mogollon, the Anasazi and the Hohokam. Their territories covered much of present-day Utah, Colorado, Arizona and New Mexico. Early settlements of these cultures consisted of shallow pit-houses that were half below ground. By AD 900 canals up to 10 miles long were being built. These provided irrigation, ensuring the harvest of two crops per year.

Islamic Conquests AD 622–945

Above. As can be seen from the map, the spread of Islam proceeded at a fast pace. The new religion had spread quickly, initially, through Arabia, and was then carried by force to outlying territories by Arab armies.

Lands conquered AD 622–632
Lands conquered AD 632–661
Lands conquered AD 661–750
Lands conquered AD 750–945

2 By AD 650 the Polynesians had reached all the major Pacific island groups, with the possible exception of New Zealand. The settlement of the Pacific islands had begun around 1000 BC and ended around AD 1000. The Polynesians were, without doubt, the world's greatest explorers and covered vast distances to reach and settle tiny islands.

direction they added Africa to their empire, defeating the Byzantines and the warlike nomads, the Berbers. By AD 700 all of Africa north of the Sahara Desert was theirs.

ISLAM IN EUROPE The sea was no obstacle: in AD 711, an army of Arabs and Berbers under the general Tariq Ibn Ziyad landed in Spain near a great rock which came to be named after him—Jebel-al-Tariq–the rock of Gibraltar. A few years later Spain was a province of Islam, called al-Andalus, the land of the Vandals, which gives us the modern name, Andalusia.

Now it was only the Franks in France and the Byzantines in Greece and Turkey who kept Islam at bay. But the empire was stretched to its limit now; it was far greater than the Arabs could control. It needed all the skills of their subject peoples–Egyptians, Syrians and Persians–and the fighting power of armies of slave soldiers to hold it together.

Because of this, when the Islamic people had conquered new territory, they administered it in a way which took account of the local culture, to keep unrest at bay.

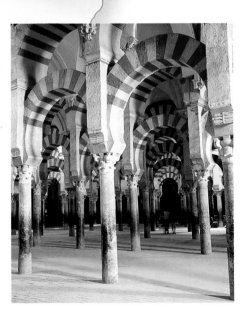

The Arab conquest of Spain led to the birth of the Moorish culture. Buildings constructed by the Moors represent some of the finest examples of Islamic architecture. This is part of the highly decorated interior of the Grand Mosque at Cordoba.

ISLAMIC SCHOLARS AND ARTISTS

A detail of the wooden panelling from the walls of a Fatimid palace from the tenth century AD.

The scene depicts two musicians. It was unusual to show the figures of human beings or animals in Islamic designs, as it was thought that only *Allah*, the god of Islam, had the right to design such figures.

Mathematicians and astronomers were also highly prized and were put to good use in surveying and agriculture.

THE TRANSLATORS The old knowledge was translated from its original Greek into Arabic, often by way of Persian or Syrian, and so it spread easily through the Empire.

In Spain, although the rulers were Muslims, Christian monasteries flourished. Islam was far more tolerant of Christianity than vice versa. Pope Sylvester III had studied in a Spanish monastery, and it was here that Greek books, now in Arabic, were translated into Latin. This is the tortuous way that learning gradually spread to France, Britain and Germany.

SIMPLE NUMBERS We take our numbers for granted. But Roman numerals, the counting system of the old Roman Empire, were very different, and difficult to use. Adding CIX to LIV to get CLXIII seems a lot more difficult than adding 109 to 54 to make 163. The latter counting system is, of course, the one we use today and is the product of Islam.

The system actually originated in India, but it was Islamic science that spread it through Europe. In fact, in the early days, these numbers were called 'algorisms,' after the ninth-century mathematician, Al-Khwarizmi. The numbering system allowed Arab scientists to do complicated calculations.

The Muslims advanced the science of astronomy, particularly by developing instruments like the *astrolabe*, which was to become an essential aid to navigation at sea.

For the thousand years before the birth of Islam, Greece and the lands influenced by the Greeks, had been the center of science and learning, and had been the intellectual center of the Roman Empire. Philosophers and mathematicians such as Aristotle, Ptolemy and Archimedes had written about the way that the world worked. Scientists such as Hippocrates and Galen had written medical textbooks.

Their works had been collected and copied by Greeks, Romans and Byzantines. But many of these scholars became branded as *heretics* at home, and fled to Persia. Here, Greek learning mixed with the science and philosophy of India and China, to reach an even more advanced state.

THE NEW SCHOLARS It was through Persia, once the bitter enemy of Greece and Rome, that a lot of the ancient wisdom was preserved. The *caliphs* brought scholars from Persia, Syria, Egypt, and all over their new empire, to the courts at Damascus and Baghdad. It mattered little to them whether the scholars were Jews, Christians or Moslems. What counted most was their learning, particularly in philosophy, science and literature.

ARCHITECTS AND ARTISTS Arab engineers and builders have left us buildings of breath-taking beauty, including mosques with tall minarets and majestic domes and cool palaces with arcaded courts. The details of the buildings are exquisite.

The Arabs used abstract patterns, especially curving 'arabesques' which might be carved, painted or inlaid. Passages from the *Qur'an* were often worked into the patterns, so that Islamic *calligraphy* became an art in itself.

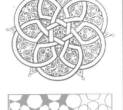

Left. The Dome of the Rock in Jerusalem, also called the Mosque of Omar, was built between AD 669–692. It covers the spot from which Mohammad is believed to have risen to heaven. It is without doubt one of the most exquisite examples of Islamic architecture. You can see how fine the abstract designs are all around the mosque. It is regarded as the most beautiful building in Jerusalem.

Above. Muslim artists were discouraged from painting people or animals. Thus, they created abstract designs and geometric patterns, such as these.

Above. A reconstruction of the *minaret* of the Great Mosque at Samarra, begun by al-Mutawakkil in AD 847. This circular minaret with a spiral ramp follows the scheme of the temple towers, or *ziggurats*, of ancient Assyria. The mosque is the largest in the Islamic world.

Famous Muslim Scholars

The early Islamic world produced a remarkable number of learned and influential scholars. There follow descriptions of some of the most famous.

Ibn Sina (known in Europe as Aricenna) was born in AD 980 near Bukhara in central Asia. He studied medicine, mathematics, astronomy, climatology and philosophy. His writings helped to spread Muslim scientific and medical knowledge to Europe. His book on medicine, entitled *al-Qanun*, was one of the most widely used medical textbooks during the Middle Ages. In it, he accurately describes the symptoms and spread of many serious diseases, and lists 760 different drugs used by Muslim physicians.

Al-Razi (known in Europe as Rhazes) was a physician in charge of the Baghdad hospital during the AD 900s. He was famous as the most skilful doctor of his generation. He developed several new and effective treatments for illnesses, and wrote a comprehensive medical encyclopedia.

Above. A detail from a page of a book on medicine. Written by a doctor in Baghdad in the eleventh century. Marrows were used to quench the thirst and cleanse the bowels.

Al-Khwarizmi lived in ninth century Khurason in central Asia. He wrote many books on mathematical topics. The word 'algebra' as used today, comes from the title of one of his books.

Al-Masudi, who lived in tenth century Egypt, studied the natural world, and wrote on geography, geology and biology. He suggested a theory of evolution, almost 900 years before Charles Darwin developed the theory in the western world. He was a great traveler and wrote a 30-volume encyclopedia describing all the countries he had visited.

Left. The astrolabe is believed to have been invented by a Greek scientist named Hipparchus in 150 BC. Islamic scholars developed the instrument, and it became the chief instrument for navigational purposes, until superseded in the fourteenth century. This astrolabe dates from about the ninth century AD.

The Eastern World
INDIA AND SOUTHEAST ASIA

While Rome ruled the west, the Kushan Empire, which lasted from AD 78–500 ruled northern India, Pakistan and Afghanistan. This was a period of great achievement and prosperity, but the explosion of barbarians which put an end to the Roman Empire also brought chaos to India.

HUNS AND ARABS The white Huns poured into India around AD 500 and the Kushan civilization was wrecked. India became a land of many kingdoms, often at war with each other. Then around AD 700 Arabs fought their way into India and the first Muslim states were founded.

Throughout this period of chaos, Indian culture carried on. Beautiful Hindu temples and statues were erected. Poets, philosophers and historians carried on writing, and Buddhism spread far afield from India to Nepal, Tibet, China, Japan and Southeast Asia.

THE GREAT PILGRIMAGE Pilgrims traveled enormous distances to India, the home of Buddhism. In the seventh century Hsuan-tsang, a Chinese Buddhist, left his home and trekked around the north of the Himalayas across deserts and mountains to reach Kanauj, the capital of the Buddhist king, Harsha, on the River Ganges in northeast India. After several years of study he returned home with a precious baggage of holy books and flower seeds; his pilgrimage had lasted for 16 years.

INTO SOUTHEAST ASIA The Romans had traded with India, during the period of the Empire, and to supply this trade Indians had explored Southeast Asia, Burma, Thailand, Malaya, Sumatra, Java and Borneo in search of gems and spices. After the traders went priests, and the great religions of India–Hinduism and Buddhism–were taken up by native peoples. Chinese traders came to the area too, and the mixture of foreign civilizations and native traditions produced a spectacular culture.

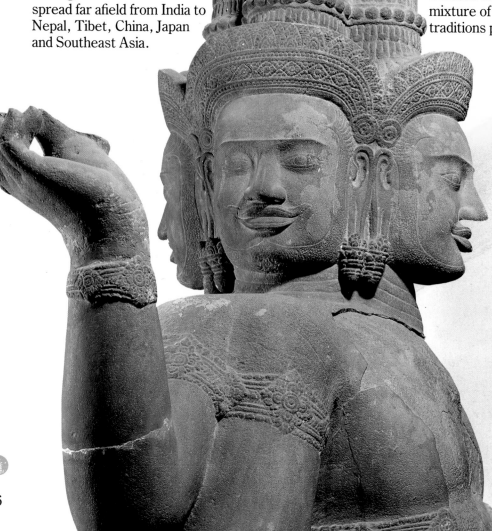

Left. This Khmer sandstone statue from the tenth century AD depicts the Hindu god, Brahma. He was considered to be the father of mankind in general, and to be the god of wisdom. This view of the statue shows three of his four heads.

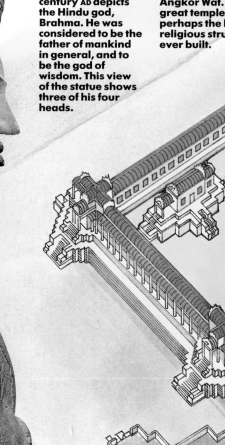

Below. This is a reconstruction of the Khmer capital of Angkor Wat. This great temple is perhaps the largest religious structure ever built.

THE KINGDOM OF THE KHMER In Cambodia the
results were particularly spectacular, and the Kingdom of
the Khmer (Cambodians) soon ruled huge areas of
Southeast Asia. Their kings conquered new lands and
seized slaves and tribute. The wealth from these
conquests can still be seen in the great cities and temples
of the Cambodian jungle.

The Khmer Kingdom began in the eighth century AD.
The Khmers built cities like Banteay Srei, large and
beautifully decorated buildings for the worship of Hindu
gods as well as for the running of the kingdom.
Eventually the Empire came to be centered at Angkor
where King Suryavarman (AD 1113–1150) built Angkor
Wat, the most splendid of all the temples, richly
decorated with carvings and towers.

RICE AND WATER Around the Khmer temples were
lakes–not just for decoration, but because the cities
depended on them. The basic food, rice, was grown in
wet paddy fields, and artificial irrigation was the only way
to bring enough water to the fields. Whole rivers were
diverted, and huge
reservoirs, one 4.2 miles
long and 1.2 miles
were created to wide,
support the great
cities of the
Khmer.

**Right. A detail of the
fine and intricate
carvings at Angkor
Thom today.**

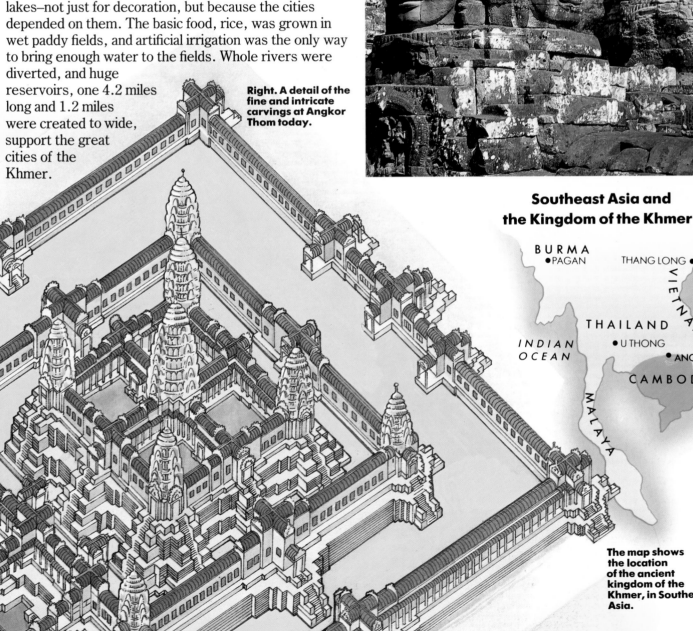

**Southeast Asia and
the Kingdom of the Khmer**

BURMA
● PAGAN
THANG LONG ●
VIETNAM
THAILAND
INDIAN
OCEAN
● U THONG
● ANGKOR
CAMBODIA
MALAYA

**The map shows
the location
of the ancient
kingdom of the
Khmer, in Southeast
Asia.**

CHINA: ANARCHY TO EMPIRE

This beautiful Tang painting of camels running through the trees is typical of the high standard of the art produced during the era of Tang dominance.

The history of China is the story of different *dynasties* coming to power and creating great empires which eventually collapsed. The Han Dynasty came to an end in AD 220, when the Roman Empire was at its peak, and after its demise, the vast land of China broke up into many small kingdoms. This lasted until AD 529 when a general, We Ti, conquered the whole country to initiate his own, Sui, Dynasty.

THE BEGINNING OF THE TANG DYNASTY By AD 618, China was again slipping into anarchy. In that year the Sui Emperor was assassinated, and Liu Yiian, the first Emperor of the Tang Dynasty, took over.

He founded a dynasty which would last until AD 907. This time was one of the peaks of Chinese civilization, marked by its art, culture and organization. After AD 907 the Empire split into warring states again until it was reunited by Chao Kwang Yin, first Emperor of the Sung Dynasty, in AD 960.

THE ALL-POWERFUL EMPEROR: The Chinese world during this period was organized to give complete power to the Emperor and his civil service. All adult men paid tax to the Emperor for their land, and some of this tax was extracted in the form of forced labor. In AD 607 more than a million men were called up to 'pay' their taxes by repairing part of the Great Wall of China; in the 20 days that they worked, many died.

The same forced labor was used to build the Grand Canal, which was used to bring food from the rice fields on the Yangtze River more than 600 miles to the capitals at Loyang and Chang'an. Roads and bridges, beautifully engineered, were also built, using forced labor, and were overseen and managed by the skilled administrators of the civil service.

Later, the Sung emperors were to devise entrance examinations to set a high academic standard for their administrators, so the role of the civil service became very important.

The Tang Empire

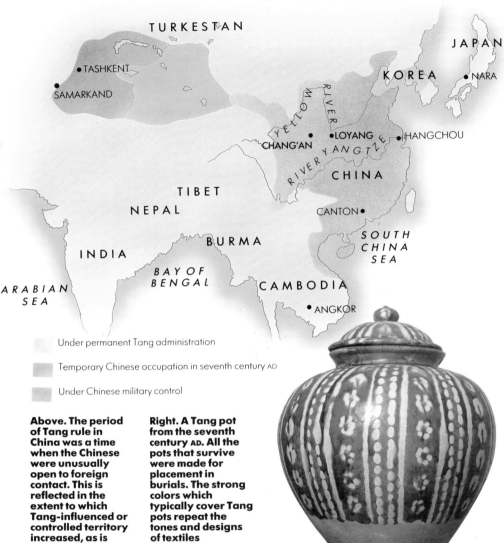

Under permanent Tang administration

Temporary Chinese occupation in seventh century AD

Under Chinese military control

Above. The period of Tang rule in China was a time when the Chinese were unusually open to foreign contact. This is reflected in the extent to which Tang-influenced or controlled territory increased, as is shown in the map.

Right. A Tang pot from the seventh century AD. All the pots that survive were made for placement in burials. The strong colors which typically cover Tang pots repeat the tones and designs of textiles fashionable at the time.

Chinese Medicine

In ancient China, medical treatment was largely based on herbal remedies. The herb Artemesia Moxa (2) was used in *moxibustion*. This treatment involved burning the herb at points directly on the skin where the pain was felt. Many other herbs were used such as mint (1), which was believed to relieve headaches.

During the Tang Dynasty, a book known as *The Tang Book on Drugs and Herbs* was written. The information in it was used as the basis of the most respected book on the subject today.

Acupuncture was also developed by the ancient Chinese. Very thin needles are painlessly inserted into specific parts of the body to relieve a wide range of illnesses. The diagram above shows the heart meridian of the acupuncture system.

TRADE WITH THE OUTSIDE WORLD Throughout its long history, China has had periods of remaining shut off to other states, and periods of welcoming communication and trade with them. During this era, China was 'open' to the west and the south, and traded freely with other countries. Silk traveled west along the Silk Road, and spices, woods, gems, and fine pottery went west by sea via India to the Persian Gulf, Egypt and Africa.

In return came gold and silver and masterpieces of art. With the trade came foreign traders, including Arabs, Jews, Persians and *Nestorian* Christians from Central Asia. They made the empire a center of international trade, with their own living areas in the capital cities of Loyang and Chang'an, and in the ports of Canton and Hangchow. China was a great hive of activity during this period, and extremely cosmopolitan.

POTS AND PAINTINGS China's own crafts flourished too; underground tombs of the Tang period had beautifully painted walls, which show how magnificent the palaces must have been. Chinese pottery was very fine and highly prized by western customers.

This Tang *rhyton*, or drinking cup, dates from the seventh century AD. It features an animal's head and is decorated with relief carvings of musicians.

59

THE SILK ROAD

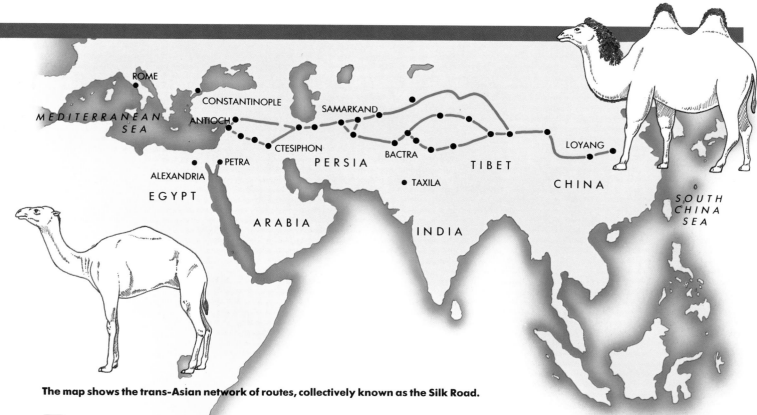

The map shows the trans-Asian network of routes, collectively known as the Silk Road.

For many centuries the wonderful silk cloth that was made only in China, had been brought thousands of miles to the Near East and Europe. The Romans had not been at all sure how it was made; they speculated that it came from a plant, but they were wrong.

After the fall of the Roman Empire, the demand for silk continued; the noble and royal families of the Arabs, Byzantines, Franks, Moors and Anglo-Saxons all delighted in the gossamer-like fabric.

THE SECRET OF SILK In the sixth century AD Persians came to the court of the Byzantine Emperor and Empress, Justinian and Theodora, and produced, from a hollow walking stick, the eggs of the silk worm. The Byzantines hatched them, and silk worms appeared as the answer to the puzzle. By unwinding the silken thread from the cocoons of these caterpillars, silk was made.

Soon the Byzantine silk works were weaving their own silk. But the finest, most luxurious, cloth still came from China.

OVER DESERTS AND MOUNTAINS The distance from the Great Wall of China to Antioch in Syria is more than 3125 miles, and the journey ranges over the deserts of Mongolia, the Pamir and Hindukush mountains, the high plateau of Iran and the rivers and deserts of Iraq. This was the overland route used for Chinese trade to Europe, known as the Silk Road. This was not a paved road like a motorway, but rather an overland track, dotted with countless caravans trudging all the way from China to Europe.

The route was formed out of a complicated chain of many links, some end-to-end and some side-by-side. Silk and other goods were shuttled from one city to the next, handled by dozens of different traders as one trader passed his commodities on to the next. It is unlikely that many traders from China ever saw Syria or Byzantium. But each trader would have had his share of rivers and deserts to cross and mountain passes to climb along the varied route.

RESTING PLACES A broad corridor of *caravanserais* (caravan depots) grew up where the caravans could stop for food and rest. These were like small walled towns, defended against attack and wild animals, and bustled with life.

THE SHIFTING ROUTES The exact route that any trader took depended on many things: the time of year was important since mountain passes might only be open in

The Heyday of the Silk Road

The first millenium AD had seen an explosion in urban development. Cities such as Chang'an and Alexandria may have had populations exceeding 500,000. These huge populations encouraged the growth of trade.

The heyday of the Silk Road was seen during the period of the Tang Dynasty in China (AD 618–906). Many remains of trade goods have been excavated along the routes. They show the great developments in art and culture that were achieved during this era.

Left. Itinerant merchants, like this Persian pedlar, traveled the Silk Road for many centuries.

Above. This fragment of silk embroidery dates from the third/fifth centuries AD. It was found on the Silk Road.

Below. The present-day ruins of Jiaohe, which was once a bustling sixth-century Silk Road city. Cities such as Jiaohe grew very wealthy during the great days of the Silk Road because they controlled trade.

the summer, and deserts were easier to cross in the winter. Politics were important too; sometimes the invasions of Huns, Arabs, Persians, and Byzantines closed parts of the route. Sometimes local rulers imposed high taxes, and a different road would have to be found to avoid them.

THE SPICE ROUTE But there was a different way: a sea route started from China, swung around Malaya to India and continued on to the Persian Gulf, the Red Sea, Egypt and even down to the east coast of Africa.

When the monsoon winds were right, Arab traders would set out from China and make colossal journeys to carry silks, spices, precious stones and woods, and pottery, which would eventually reach the markets of Africa, Europe and Middle East. The sea route would be full of dangers, such as storms and pirates. However, its advantage over the Silk Road was that many more goods could be carried on a ship than on a camel. Both the Silk Road and the Spice Route were to endure through much of history as the most important routes of trade and communication between East and West.

JAPAN

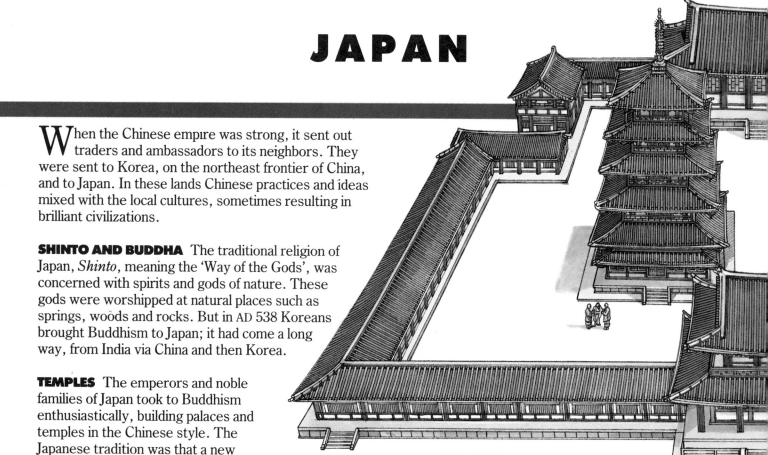

When the Chinese empire was strong, it sent out traders and ambassadors to its neighbors. They were sent to Korea, on the northeast frontier of China, and to Japan. In these lands Chinese practices and ideas mixed with the local cultures, sometimes resulting in brilliant civilizations.

SHINTO AND BUDDHA The traditional religion of Japan, *Shinto*, meaning the 'Way of the Gods', was concerned with spirits and gods of nature. These gods were worshipped at natural places such as springs, woods and rocks. But in AD 538 Koreans brought Buddhism to Japan; it had come a long way, from India via China and then Korea.

TEMPLES The emperors and noble families of Japan took to Buddhism enthusiastically, building palaces and temples in the Chinese style. The Japanese tradition was that a new palace, and a new royal temple, was built in honor of each new emperor. Thus Japan, even today, has a huge variety of large temples, each one a collection of finely built wooden structures clustered in a courtyard. Some, like the Horyuji temple shown here, have lasted for nearly 1500 years.

MONASTERIES The temples also served as monasteries. The monks who served the temples as priests lived in dormitories outside the courtyard. Inside the monastery was a Main Hall, filled with statues of the Buddha and Buddhist deities, which was used on ceremonial occasions. There was also a Sutra Hall where sacred books were kept, and a *Pagoda*. This tall, many-roofed tower contained holy relics, often bones of the Buddha or a saint. Many pilgrims would travel to the monasteries to worship.

TOMBS Buddhism did not take over in every part of life in Japan. In some aspects the old ways lingered on, especially in death.

The proper Buddhist burial was cremation: the body was burned, the ashes put in a pot or a metal container, and eventually buried in the ground. But the old Japanese style was very different. Tombs were dug into the hillside like tunnels, or built of huge stones and buried under artificial hills. The bodies were placed inside,

Key Dates in Early Japan

AD 258 or 318	'Emperor' Sujin, probably first chief of federated tribes under the Yamato
AD 300	Spread of wet-rice agriculture to whole of Japan, except Hokkaido
AD 475	Consolidation of Yamato state under horse-riding nobles
AD 538 or 552	Buddhism introduced into Japan from China
AD 607	First Horyuji Temple built
AD 670	First Horyuji Temple destroyed by fire
AD 708	Copper and silver coins officially minted
AD 710	Beginning of the Nara period. Japan becomes a centralized state based on the Chinese system of administration.

intact, and the entrance was blocked. Inside the walls of the tombs were sometimes painted, and pots, beads, buckles and other everyday objects placed with the body.

HOUSES AND PEOPLE In ordinary towns and villages the Japanese lived in wooden houses, simple versions of the great halls of the temples. Here they lived their lives as farmers, craftsmen and traders. They worshipped the old spirits of Shinto and the new gods of Buddhism.

The influence of China had improved their lives, but they were still free to live in their own culture and were not ruled by Chinese masters.

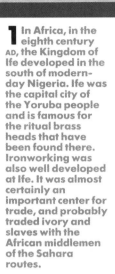

Left. The Horyuji temple complex at Nara, Japan. The temple was originally built in AD 607, but was destroyed by fire in AD 670. It was rebuilt 20 years later. All temple complexes in early Japan were composed of the same elements. Here you can see the pagoda (center courtyard, left); the main hall (center courtyard, right); the lecture hall (center, top); the middle gate (center, bottom); and the cloisters (surrounding the courtyard).

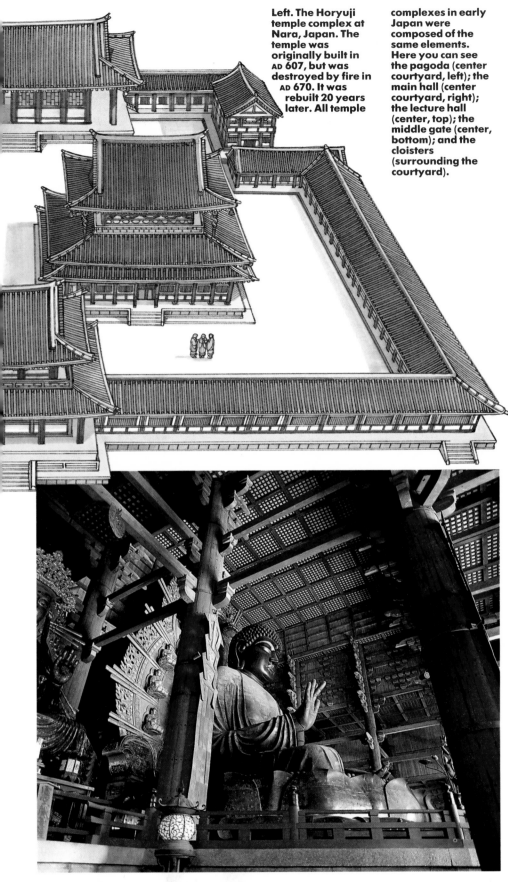

Japanese Buddhist Monks

The drawing below shows an early typical Japanese monk. Then, as now, the way of living adopted by a monk was harsh.

They want nothing for themselves and live with only what they actually need. They are dependent on people giving them food, but must not ask for it themselves.

Monks eat only one meal a day and this must be over before midday. This gives them the rest of the day for meditation, study, teaching and practical tasks.

1 In Africa, in the eighth century AD, the Kingdom of Ife developed in the south of modern-day Nigeria. Ife was the capital city of the Yoruba people and is famous for the ritual brass heads that have been found there. Ironworking was also well developed at Ife. It was almost certainly an important center for trade, and probably traded ivory and slaves with the African middlemen of the Sahara routes.

2 Around AD 800, the Dorset culture of the Inuit people of the Arctic thrived. This people made great advances in the development of the Inuit culture. Their settlements grew larger, and half-underground winter houses have been unearthed which would have held between two and three families. The people fished and hunted sea mammals and caribou with improved spears and harpoon-heads. In a short space of time, and for unclear reasons, this culture had completely disappeared by around AD 1000.

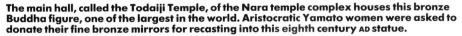

The main hall, called the Todaiji Temple, of the Nara temple complex houses this bronze Buddha figure, one of the largest in the world. Aristocratic Yamato women were asked to donate their fine bronze mirrors for recasting into this eighth century AD statue.

The Americas and Beyond
SETTLING THE PACIFIC

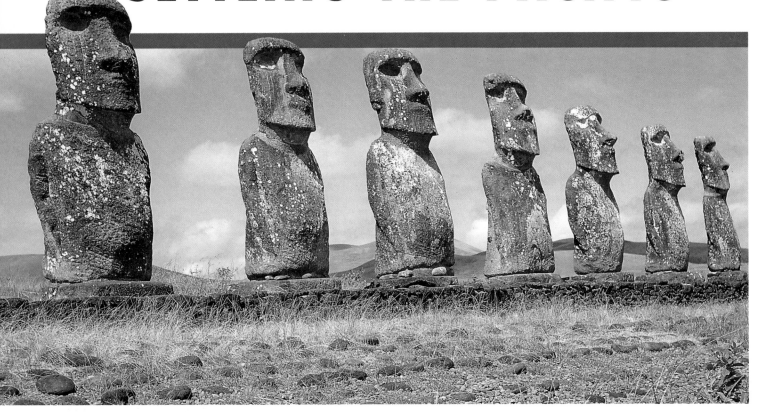

The inhabitants of Easter Island carved and erected a huge number of stone statues. All the statues on the island were pushed over face downward in the late eighteenth and nineteenth centuries. But these at Ahu Akivi have been re-erected.

The East Indies and Pacific islands nearest to Australia, Micronesia and Melanesia, were settled very early. But between 2000–1000 BC a new people began to move eastward through the settled islands. They had originally come from the coasts and islands of Southeast Asia, and by 1000 BC they had reached Samoa and Tonga, islands on the western edge of Polynesia, where archaeologists have found remains of their villages, with distinctive tools and pottery.

THE WIDE OCEAN Here they paused in their progress for more than 1000 years, and no wonder. Ahead of them lay the Pacific Ocean, 6,000 miles across, with islands scattered across it, some of them hundreds of miles apart. Exploration was dangerous and uncertain, but around AD 300 Polynesians began to spread east, and settled the main island groups, the Society Islands and the Marquesas Islands.

Imagine what the voyage must have been like. Men and women set out on journeys of 1000–2000 miles across the open sea in dug-out canoes containing their families and everything that was needed for a new life in a new land–seeds, plants, animals, tools–everything.

Polynesian Tools and Jewelry

All the above artifacts were found in the Pacific islands. Adze with carved handle (1); amulets of whale ivory (2); perforated tooth pendants (3); fishhook of pearl shell (4); necklace of tooth and bones (5).

The early Polynesians abandoned the making of pottery in the first millenium AD, and metallurgy never reached the Pacific islands beyond western New Guinea.

Despite this, the archaeological remains which exist are rich and varied, and show us much about early Polynesian life. Most tools and jewelry were made from stone, bone, shell and whale ivory. Some of the carvings which survive are very ornate and show a high level of craftsmanship.

64

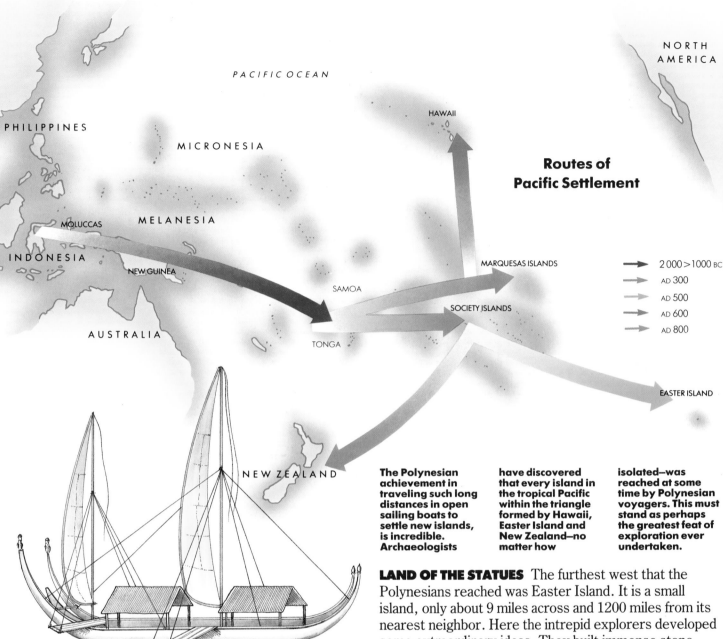

PACIFIC OCEAN

NORTH AMERICA

PHILIPPINES

MICRONESIA

HAWAII

Routes of Pacific Settlement

MELANESIA

MOLUCCAS

INDONESIA

NEW GUINEA

MARQUESAS ISLANDS

SAMOA

SOCIETY ISLANDS

AUSTRALIA

TONGA

EASTER ISLAND

→	2 000 > 1000 BC
→	AD 300
→	AD 500
→	AD 600
→	AD 800

NEW ZEALAND

Above. The boats used by the Polynesians for their long voyages, possibly looked something like this reconstruction.

The Polynesian achievement in traveling such long distances in open sailing boats to settle new islands, is incredible. Archaeologists have discovered that every island in the tropical Pacific within the triangle formed by Hawaii, Easter Island and New Zealand—no matter how isolated—was reached at some time by Polynesian voyagers. This must stand as perhaps the greatest feat of exploration ever undertaken.

EASTER ISLAND AND HAWAII By AD 500 they had reached Easter Island, halfway to South America, and 100 years later they had reached the islands of Hawaii, far to the north. The distances they traveled were far in advance of any sea journeys undertaken by other peoples up to this point in history.

THE NEW HOMES On their new islands they grew *yams*, bananas, sweet potatoes, coconuts and *breadfruit*, and collected fish and shellfish from the sea. The rest of their meat came from the domestic animals that they had brought in their canoes–pigs, dogs, hens and rats. They built temples on stone platforms, and thatched wooden houses on land where building materials and food were easy to find.

LAND OF THE STATUES The furthest west that the Polynesians reached was Easter Island. It is a small island, only about 9 miles across and 1200 miles from its nearest neighbor. Here the intrepid explorers developed some extraordinary ideas. They built immense stone platforms, and on them they raised huge stone statues, up to 33 feet high and 88 tons in weight. For a people whose culture did not yet embrace the technology of metals and who had not developed the wheel, this was a colossal achievement.

THE COLD SOUTH The last great migration of the Polynesians was to the south, to the two islands of New Zealand, which they reached around AD 800 or 900. This was a different land from the rest; not a tropical paradise, but cooler and wetter.

Here the Polynesians, better known as *Maoris*, changed their way of life to suit the new environment. Most of their traditional crops died out, but sweet potatoes flourished, and sea food was plentiful. There were giant birds, called moas, which were hunted for meat in the forest. The Maoris had found a different sort of Pacific paradise.

AFRICA: SOUTH OF THE SAHARA

CHRISTIAN KINGDOMS When the Arabs spread so quickly across North Africa it was the Sahara Desert that stopped them spreading to the south, except in the case of Egypt. Here the rich valley of the Nile acts like a highway into the mountains of Sudan and Ethiopia. In the south of Sudan the Arabs were stopped by the kingdom of Nubia around Meroë; here were African Christians who had been converted by Byzantine missionaries in the 550s and 560s.

Right. This bronze casting of a human head comes from Igbo Ukwu in southeast Nigeria. The people of this culture produced some marvelous bronze statues, quite distinct in style from bronzes produced in other African states. This bronze dates from the ninth century AD.

Sub-Saharan Trade

TUNIS
FEZ
TAGHAZA
NUBIA
MEROË
GHANA
KUMBI SALEH
TIMBUKTU
GAO
BAMBUK
JENNE-JENO
MALI
IFE
IGBO UKWU
ATLANTIC OCEAN
MOGADISHU

→ Trade routes

This map shows the routes by which trade goods were carried across the Sahara and down the east coast. The cities founded on and around such routes developed the richest cultures.

To the south of Nubia, and closer to the Red Sea was Axum, a kingdom which lived partly by trade across the Red Sea with Arabia. In fact, about 500 BC people from south Arabia had crossed over to Ethiopia, and this mixture of African and Arabian cultures produced a rich and exotic civilization. Axum is most famous for the huge stone *stelae*, or columns, set up over royal burials around AD 400. Soon after this, Greek and Syrian missionaries converted the people of Axum to Christianity, setting up a rival church to the Nubian one but one that still flourishes in Ethiopia today.

These kingdoms resisted the Islamic Arab expansion of the seventh century AD, but the trade routes of the Red Sea came under Arab control. Axum and Nubia were almost cut off from the outside world.

GREAT GHANA On the other side of Africa another kingdom was growing. The Arabs called it Ghana, but it should not be confused with the country which we call Ghana today. The ancient kingdom was called Wagadu by its people and encompassed the region where Mali and Mauretania are situated today. To begin with it was a tribe of farmers in the *savannah*–the plains south of the Sahara Desert. But in the eighth and ninth centuries AD *Berber* merchants from North Africa crossed the Sahara with their camel *caravans*.

At Kumbi, on the southern edge of the Sahara, trade goods were unloaded from the desert camels and taken over by donkeys or human porters to be carried south over the savannah. In this way the city became rich on the trade. Gold from the mines of Bambuk, and ivory, skins and slaves were sold on to the cities of the Middle East. In return the Berbers brought copper to be made into ornaments, and salt. Before long Kumbi was a rich

Archaeological Remains at Igbo Ukwu

Left. A reconstruction of the burial at Igbo Ukwu.

Above. A view from above the burial pit, showing the positions in which the bones and artifacts were found.

Left. This bronze casting of an animal's head was found at Igbo Ukwu. Most of the bronzes found there are very elaborately decorated, even such everyday objects as pots, bowls and sword handles.

The Igbo Ukwu culture was only discovered relatively recently. A man was digging in his back garden for mud to build a new house. What he found were the remains of an ancient culture previously unheard of. Very little is known about the Igbo Ukwu people. From their remains it seems that they must have lived in a rich and sophisticated society which had surpluses to exchange for copper. Among the findings were beads from India, making it clear that these people engaged in long-distance trade.

The most remarkable find at Igbo Ukwu was the burial of a priest or ruler (see illustrations above). He was buried in a seated position in a wooden chamber along with his slaves. His foot was resting on an elephant tusk and a staff was placed in his right hand.

The bronzes left behind by these people are also remarkable. They are highly decorated and show an advanced technical skill, as well as a strong artistic sense.

city, with a royal palace and a special area of merchants' houses. It came to an end in the 11th century when Berbers from the desert invaded Ghana and converted it to Islam.

IGBO UKWU Further east, in the forests of Nigeria, the copper from the Sahara was being turned into wonderful ornaments for kings. At Igbo Ukwu an astonishing collection of bronze vessels and ornaments of the ninth century AD have been discovered. Close by was the burial site of a man seated on a stool in all his finery.

1 Early in the AD 800s, the Vikings of Scandinavia began to expand into Russia. They seized parts of northern Russia in the AD 860s and founded the city of Novgorod. During the same period, the Vikings launched a series of attacks on England. Between AD 856–875 they conquered the Kingdoms of Mercia, Northumbria and East Anglia.

2 The Chola Dynasty became pre-eminent in India in the ninth century AD. The early part of their rule saw a great expansion in temple-building. During this period temples in the countryside became the social and economic centers of the community, and also acted as banks and schools. The Chola Dynasty came to an end in the twelfth century AD.

3 The Abbasid Caliphs took over as rulers of the Islamic world from AD 750. During their reign, architecture and the arts flourished and a new capital was founded at Baghdad in AD 766.

THE PEOPLE OF AMERICA: HUNTERS AND GARDENERS

Hunting the Buffalo

Though North American Indians hunted many animals, the buffalo was the most important. They used every bit of it for something. As soon as the animals had been killed, men, women and children joined in skinning and cutting up the carcasses.

Spoons (1) were made from horn. Stone hammers (2) were bound to their handles with *rawhide*. Skulls (3) were painted and used in religious festivals. Bone knives (4) and bone fleshing tools (5) were made from leg bones. *Parfleches* (6), envelopes used for carrying belongings, and cases (7) for storing war bonnets were made from *rawhide*. Hide was also decorated and used to make robes (8). Finally, the tail was used as a decoration on quillwork; this served as a tent ornament.

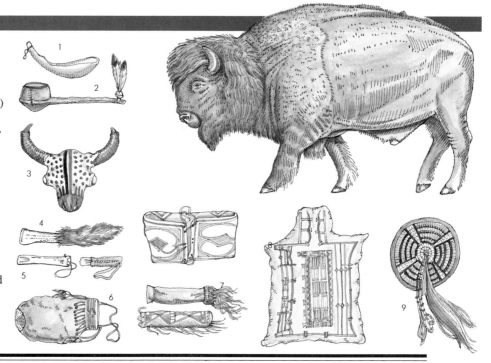

Some time in the last Ice Age, perhaps as long as 30,000 years ago, people first came into the vast continent of America.

OVER THE FROZEN WASTES The glaciers of the Arctic held so much of the world's water that the seas were 160 feet lower than they are now. What is now the Bering Strait, between Siberia and Alaska, was dry land.

Tundra stretched from Europe, through Asia, to America, and enormous herds of musk ox, bison, reindeer and horse roamed across it. Behind the herds were human hunters, and by following the herds they drifted into America. Soon they began to move south into warmer lands, through Canada into the United States and finally into South America. It was not a great migration; it was a very gradual process, tribes moving a little further each year and taking advantage of new hunting grounds. By 10,000 BC the whole of America, right down to Patagonia at the southernmost tip of the continent, was peopled by hunters.

THE LAND GROWS WARMER As the Ice Age died and the glaciers shrank, the environment changed. Forests spread over what had been endless tundra and deserts grew up where there had been forests.

The animals changed too; mammoth, horse and Arctic bison died out, to be replaced by deer, smaller bison and other species that were better adapted for the warmer climate. The hunters adapted too, and developed a new way of life.

HUNTERS TO FARMERS The first Americans brought domestic dogs with them, but it was many centuries before farming appeared in the continent. It was Central America and tropical South America where people started to grow their own food 7000–8000 years ago.

Some of the world's most important foods were cultivated here–potatoes, beans, marrows, peppers, sweet potatoes and maize. Cotton was grown for cloth and some native animals were domesticated, such as the llama, macaw, turkey and guinea pig. The llama's wool and the meat of the guinea pig were particularly important in South America.

In North America farming, which in its earliest state was actually more like gardening, caught on slowly. By 2000 BC the idea of growing maize, beans and squashes had come in from Mexico, but hunting continued to be an important way of getting food. Villagers grew their crops in gardens at home while they hunted deer, rabbits and birds in the forests. The horse had died out, so all hunting was done on foot. One plant was grown which was no use at all for food or clothing–tobacco. Smoking was an important ritual, carried out at ceremonies and festivals.

Routes of Migration into the Americas

This map shows the route the first Americans took to reach the American continent. The part of the world they crossed is now filled by sea and can only be crossed by boat: it is called the Bering Strait. Arriving as small bands of hunters, these people can have had no idea that they were, in fact, discovering a continent.

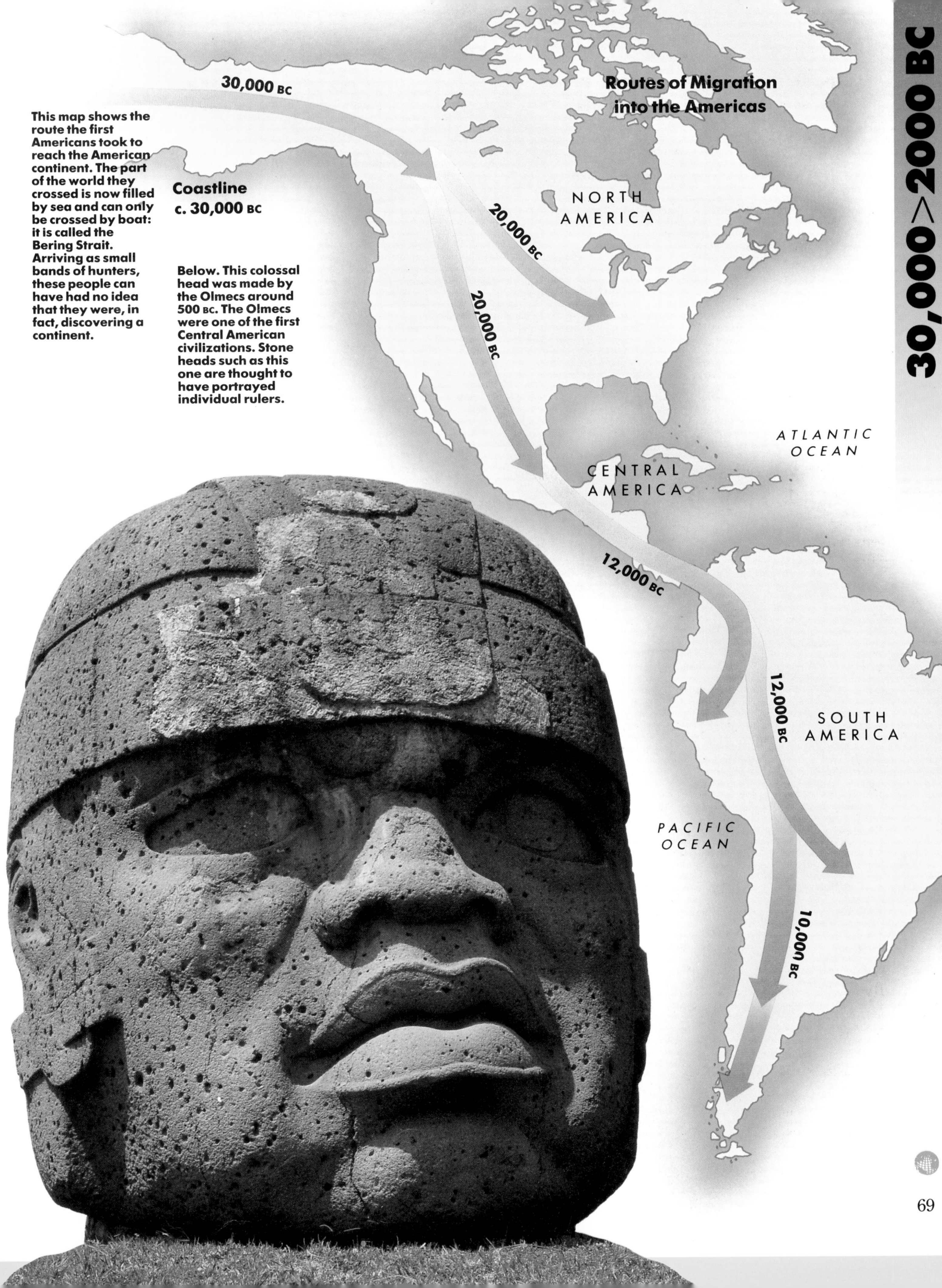

Coastline c. 30,000 BC

Below. This colossal head was made by the Olmecs around 500 BC. The Olmecs were one of the first Central American civilizations. Stone heads such as this one are thought to have portrayed individual rulers.

30,000 BC

20,000 BC

20,000 BC

NORTH AMERICA

ATLANTIC OCEAN

CENTRAL AMERICA

12,000 BC

12,000 BC

SOUTH AMERICA

PACIFIC OCEAN

10,000 BC

69

THE PEOPLE OF AMERICA: CITIES AND TEMPLES

The Maya Civilization

NORTH AMERICA

GULF OF MEXICO

● CHICHEN ITZA

CARIBBEAN SEA

● TIKAL

● PALENQUE

● COPAN

PACIFIC OCEAN

Above. Though the Mayan civilization covered a relatively small area, it probably developed the most advanced culture of the ancient American civilizations.

Right. This Mayan sculpture depicts a human face emerging from the jaws of an animal. You can see the animal's tongue hanging below the man's chin.

Even now, after many years of research, the beginning of cities and of civilization is still a mystery. Some ordinary farming villages grew into vast cities with thousands of inhabitants and specialist groups of citizens like priests, craftsmen and civil servants. This process happened at different periods in different parts of the world.

In the Americas, the first cities appeared in the jungles of Central America and on the mountains of Peru and Bolivia in South America, in about 1000 BC

THE OLMECS In Central America the first cities were built by a civilization called the *Olmecs*, between about 1000 BC and 400 BC. They were centered around stone temples where the Olmecs worshipped their jaguar gods. Why their cities died out we do not know, but there was a gap of about 400 years before the great cities of the *Maya* appeared.

Right. The Mayan city of Copan was one of the three or four main centers of the Classic Mayan civilization. Large architectural complexes such as this incorporated temples, palaces, plazas and ball

courts. Such complexes formed the centers of Mayan cities, and were fundamental to their civilization.

MAYAN CITIES A Mayan city like Copan shown here was not at all like a modern one. There were no wheeled vehicles and the cities housed only relatively small populations. The heart of the city did not consist of shops or a market, but of squares, or plazas, surrounded by high stone pyramids. Unlike Egyptian pyramids, the Mayan constructions were not intended for burials, but served as huge platforms on which temples were built.

Between the pyramids citizens gathered for festivals, ceremonies and dancing, and to watch ceremonial ball games played in great stone-walled courtyards.

MAYAN ASTRONOMERS The houses of the city were scattered around the center, still in uncleared jungle, but it was the plazas that were important. Here Mayan priests studied the sky and developed a sophisticated astronomical calendar. One of their hieroglyphic inscriptions records an astronomical conference held at Copan in AD 776.

TEMPLES OF TIHUANACO In the high Bolivian Andes, about 1300 feet above sea level, is Tihuanaco, another great city of temples, courtyards and houses. Stone pillars and statues stand in courtyards decorated with carved human heads. Around the city 20,000 acres of land were farmed, irrigated by artificial water channels, to feed the potters, priests, metalworkers, weavers and administrators who lived in the great city.

NORTH AMERICA Many of the ideas from Mexican cities traveled north into the United States. Along the Mississippi River, square mounds of

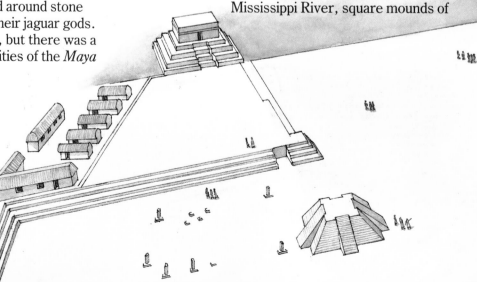

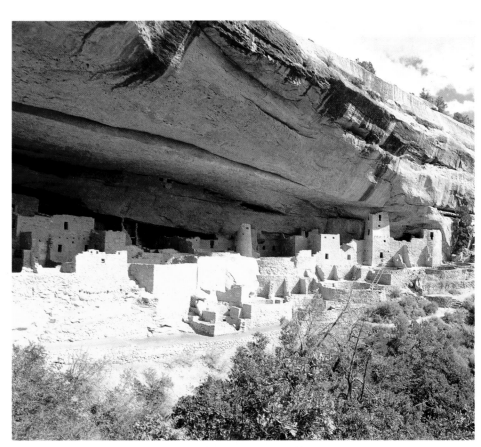

The Mayan System of Numbers

0 1 3 5 12 18

The Maya were the only truly literate civilization of the Americas. They devised a system of numbers, a calendar, and a writing system. They used three basic symbols for numbers: a shell for zero, a dot for one, and a bar for five.

Left. The dwellings at Mesa Verde in the southwest United States were built in the twelfth century AD by the Anasazi people. Of the many ruins, Cliff Palace, shown here, is the largest and most famous. It contains over 400 rooms and is four stories high in some places. The rooms were small with low ceilings.

Some rooms seem to have been entered through the roof, by using ladders, rather than by doors. No one is sure what the towers were used for at Cliff Palace. They could possibly have been defensive lookouts, or perhaps observatories for viewing the position of the sun.

earth with wooden temples appeared, that were very much like Mayan cities.

But most spectacular of all North American early towns are the towns in the deserts of the southwest of the United States. In Mesa Verde in Colorado, North American Indians built huge terraced houses in the shelter of the *mesa's* overhanging cliffs. These cliff

dwellings housed hundreds of people. The people of Mesa Verde were farmers and traces of their fields can still be seen on top of the mesa.

Five hundred years before Columbus set foot in America, native Americans had achieved much that was equivalent to what their contemporaries had achieved in Europe.

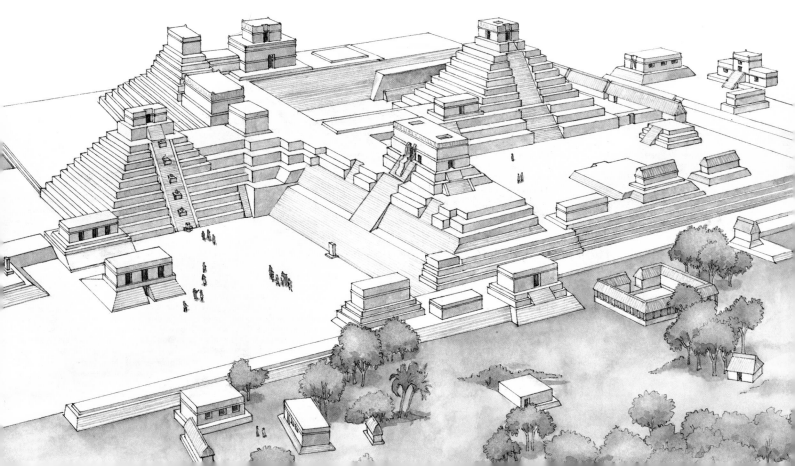

	BYZANTIUM/AFRICA	THE ISLAMIC WORLD	THE FAR EAST	AMERICA AND THE PACIFIC
AD				
320			Chandragupta founds Gupta Empire in north India	
330	Foundation of Constantinople (Byzantium)			
400	First towns appear in sub-Saharan Africa			
440	Huns in Greece			Polynesians settle in the Pacific islands
480			Gupta Empire overthrown	
500				Teotihuacan in Central America is sixth largest city in the world (population: 200,000)
529	Justinian becomes Emperor of Byzantium			
538	Silk worms brought to Constantinople			
550			Buddhism comes to Japan	
570		Muhammad born in Mecca		
589			Sui Dynasty begins in China	
622		The Hegira—Muhammad flees to Medina		
630		Muhammad captures Mecca	Tang Dynasty begins in China	
632		Muhammad dies		
641	Arabs conquer Egypt and spread into north Africa			
650		Persia invaded		All major island groups of the Pacific settled by Polynesians
660		Beginning of the Umayyad Dynasty		
700				The civilization of the Maya flourishes in Central America Domination of North American southeast by Mogollon, Hohokam and Anasazi cultures
710			Beginning of Nara period in Japan	
711		Invasion of Spain		
750		Muslims defeat Chinese army Umayyads overthrown by the Abbasid Dynasty. Capital of the Empire is moved from Damascus to Baghdad		
784			Beginning of the Heian period in Japan	
800	The civilization at Great Ghana in Africa flourishes		The Khmer Kingdom emerges in Cambodia	First use of the bow and arrow in the Mississippi valley
900	Civilization at Igbo Ukwu in Africa			Polynesians reach New Zealand
909		Fatimid Dynasty emerges in the Eastern Maghreb. Begins to compete with the Abbasids		
950				Toltecs rise to power in central Mexico
960			Sung Dynasty begins in China	
1050			Printing with moveable type invented in China	

GLOSSARY

acupuncture   A system of medicine, originating in China, where the skin is punctured with needles at particular points in order to cure illness or relieve pain.

amphorae   Huge pottery jars used to transport and store wine, olive oil, etc.

aqueduct   An overground water channel, often raised on arches over rivers, ravines and river basins.

astrolabe   An ancient instrument used for calculating the position of the sun and the stars.

barbarians   The name used by the Romans for anyone who was not Roman or did not speak Latin.

bard   A poet or singer.

Berbers   A nomadic tribe that inhabited northwestern Africa.

Buddhism   A religion founded by Siddhartha Gautama, who died in c.483 BC. Buddhists believe that the universe works according to principles that cannot be altered by men or gods.

Burgundians   One of the "barbarian" tribes that attacked the Roman Empire. They moved into eastern France and established a kingdom there around AD 480.

caliphs   The successors of Muhammad; the rulers and religious leaders of the Islamic world.

calligraphy   The art of beautiful writing.

caravan   A group of people, usually traders, travelling together for security, especially in the deserts.

caravanserai   A staging-post on a camel caravan route where rest and refreshment were available.

cavalry   The part of an army that is made up of soldiers on horseback.

civil war   A war between citizens of the same state.

Coptic   A sect of Christianity which broke away from the mainstream Church in AD 451. Other independent sects eventually developed out of the Coptic Church, including the Nestorian and Armenian Churches.

Cyrillic alphabet   The Slavonic alphabet formed in the ninth century AD, believed to have been developed by St Cyril.

Danelaw   The parts of England that the Vikings ruled.

dynasty   A family who rule a country or empire, passing power on from generation to generation.

epic poems   Long narrative poems that tell the stories of heroic events in a style of detailed description.

feudalism   A way of organizing society, stretching from one powerful, wealthy person down to those with no power at all, in which land is granted in return for military or labor services.

frankincense   A sweet-smelling resin from Arabia, used as incense.

Franks   One of the "barbarian" Germanic tribes that attacked the Roman Empire. They settled in Gaul (France) and are the ancestors of the French.

Goths   One of the "barbarian" Germanic tribes that attacked the Roman Empire. They went on to found kingdoms in Italy, southern France and Spain.

heathen   A word used by followers of the Christian or Islamic religions to describe someone who does not share their beliefs.

hegira   The word used to describe the flight of Muhammad from Mecca in AD 622. The date marks the beginning of the Muslim era.

heretic   A member of a religious group who believes something that is opposed to the authorized teaching of that religion.

Hinduism   An eastern religion with no known founder or date of founding. Hindus worship vast numbers of deities and many animals and plants are sacred to them.

hippodrome   A stadium for chariot racing.

Huns   A savage, nomadic Asian race that overran Europe under their leader, Attila, who ruled from AD 433–53.

illuminated manuscripts   Highly decorated, hand-written, hand-made books. They began to be produced in the middle of the Dark Ages and were usually made by clergymen.

Islam   The Muslim religion founded by Muhammad.

Lindisfarne Gospels   Richly illuminated Bibles produced in the late seventh century AD on the island of Lindisfarne, off the northeast coast of England.

Lombards   One of the "barbarian" tribes that attacked the Roman Empire. They eventually settled in northern Italy.

Maoris   Descendants of the Polynesian tribes who first settled in New Zealand.

mercenaries   Soliders hired for money to fight in the service of countries of which they are not citizens.

mesa   A table-shaped hill.

minaret   The tower of a mosque from which the call to prayer is given in the religion of Islam.

Moor   A person of mixed Arab/ Berber descent. The Moors conquered and occupied Spain from AD 711–1492.

mosaic   Floor or wall decoration made up of many very small fragments (called *tesserae*) of stone, tile or glass. Complicated patterns and pictures could be made in mosaic form.

Muslim A follower of the religion of Islam.

Nestorian A form of Christianity founded by Nestorius, the patriarch (chief bishop), of Constantinople from AD 428–31.

Olmecs An early culture of Central America. The Olmec civilization existed from 1200–300 BC.

Ostrogoths One of the "barbarian" tribes that attacked Rome. They settled in parts of Italy.

pagan A word used by followers of a religion to describe someone who does not share their beliefs.

pagoda A Buddhist temple tower of several stories, typically found in southeast Asia.

parfleche A receptacle made from dried buffalo skin.

pilgrimage A journey undertaken by people from many religions to a holy shrine or other holy place. For instance, Muslims typically make at least one pilgrimage to Mecca during their lifetimes.

plague An epidemic disease that can be caught by people from fleas that live on rats.

Qur'an The collection of holy scriptures of the religion of Islam.

rawhide Untanned leather.

relics When associated with the Christian religion, relics are objects (sometimes parts of the body) thought to have belonged to saints or other people of religious significance.

rhyton A drinking cup or pottery horn with a hole in the point to drink through.

Romance languages General name for the modern languages that developed out of the Latin spoken throughout Europe during the era of the Roman Empire. French, Spanish, Italian, Portuguese and Romanian are all Romance languages.

runes A system of writing consisting of simple strokes, devised by Germanic people in the third century AD. Runes were used throughout northern Europe during the Dark Ages as a result of Viking expansion.

Rus Vikings who settled on the trade route between Novgorod and Kiev in the ninth century AD. The name "Russia" comes from the Rus.

sack To plunder or devastate a town.

scribe A professional writer, employed to write letters, keep accounts and make copies of books. A scribe might also keep a record of events.

Shinto The name given to a wide variety of religious practices which developed in prehistoric Japan. In its simplest form it broadly believes that there is a supernatural living form in all natural objects, such as mountains, trees and animals.

stelae Standing pillars of stone with inscriptions carved on them.

Sutra hall The building in a Japanese Buddhist temple complex where the scriptures are kept.

tundra An Arctic plain. The vegetation is mainly mosses, lichens and stunted shrubs.

Varangians Vikings who pushed as far south as Constantinople. Many of them took service as mercenaries in the Byzantine army.

Vikings A Scandinavian people who raided, traded with and settled in many parts of Europe beween the eighth and eleventh centuries AD.

Visigoths One of the "barbarian" tribes that attacked the Roman Empire. They went on to settle areas of France and all of Spain.

yam A large vegetable like the potato.

Zoroastrianism An ancient Persian religion founded by the prophet Zoroaster.

INDEX

Further Reading

GENERAL REFERENCE

The Roman Empire and the Dark Ages: History of Everyday Things by Giovanni Caselli (Bedrick, Peter, 1985)

In Search of the Dark Ages by Michael Wood (Facts On File, 1987)

The Penguin Atlas of Medieval History by Colin McEvedy (Viking Pengiun, 1986)

EUROPE

Everyday Life of the Barbarians: Goths, Franks, and Vandals by Malcolm Todd (Hippocrene, 1988)

The Vikings: Fact and Fiction by Robin Place (Cambridge U., 1987)

The Vikings by Pamela Odijk (Silver Burdett, 1990)

Viking Warriors by Tony Triggs (Watts, Franklin, 1991)

THE REST OF THE WORLD

Lost Cities of Africa by Basil Davidson (Little, Brown, 1988)

Africa in History by Basil Davidson (Macmillan, 1992)

A Concise History of India by Francis Watson (Thames & Hudson, 1979)

China: Great Civilizations by Beth McKillop (Watts, Franklin, 1988)

Japan: Great Civilizations by Mavis Pilbeam (Watts, Franklin, 1988)

Japan: Early History (Raintree Steck-Vaughn, 1991)

Picture Acknowledgements

The author and publishers would like to acknowledge, with thanks,
the following photographic sources:
Front cover (left and right) Werner Forman Archive; p. 10 C.M. Dixon; p. 11 Ancient Art &
Architecture Collection; p. 12 Barbara Heller Photo Library; p. 13 (left) Ancient Art &
Architecture Collection, (right) C.M. Dixon; p. 15 Ancient Art & Architecture Collection;
p. 17 (upper left) Sonia Halliday Photographs, (upper right) Werner Forman Archive, (lower)
C.M. Dixon; p. 19 (left) SCALA, (right) C.M. Dixon; p. 20 (left) AKG, (right) Ancient Art &
Architecture Collection; p. 21 (all photos) Stanley E. West; p. 22 AKG; p. 25 (upper and lower)
Ancient Art & Architecture Collection; p. 26 (upper) Werner Forman Archive, (centre) C.M.
Dixon; p. 27 AKG; p. 28 SCALA; p. 29 Sonia Halliday Photographs; p. 31 Sonia Halliday
Photographs; p. 32 SCALA; p. 34 (upper and lower left) Ancient Art & Architecture Collection,
(centre) Werner Forman Archive; p. 36 Werner Forman Archive; p. 37 Werner Forman
Archive; p. 38 (upper) Michael Holford, (lower) Ancient Art & Architecture Collection;
p. 39 (upper left) The British Library, (upper right) Ashmolean Museum, Oxford, (lower)
Michael Holford; p. 42 (upper) Robert Harding Picture Library, (lower) Sonia Halliday
Photographs; p. 44 Sonia Halliday Photographs; p. 45 Sonia Halliday Photographs; p. 46 (upper)
Robert Harding Picture Library, (lower) C.M. Dixon; p. 47 (upper left and right) C.M. Dixon,
(lower) Michael Holford; p. 48 (upper) C.M. Dixon, (lower) Ancient Art & Architecture
Collection; p. 50 Ancient Art & Architecture Collection; p. 51 The Chester Beatty Library;
p. 52 (upper) Ancient Art & Architecture Collection, (lower) Réunion des Musées National;
p. 53 Sonia Halliday Photographs; p. 54 C.M. Dixon; p. 55 (upper) Robert Harding Picture
Library, (middle) Österreichische Nationalbibliothek, Vienna, (lower) William MacQuitty;
p. 56 Michael Holford; p. 57 Robert Harding Picture Library; p. 58 William MacQuitty;
p. 59 (upper and lower) Ancient Art & Architecture Collection; p. 61 (upper) Ancient Art &
Architecture Collection, (lower) Robert Harding Picture Library; p. 63 Werner Forman Archive;
p. 64 Ancient Art & Architecture Collection; pp. 66 and 67 Trustees of the British Museum;
p. 69 Werner Forman Archive; p. 70 Michael Holford; p. 71 Werner Forman Archive.